Two week loan

ACCOUNTANTS' LIABILITY IN THE 1980s

CROOM HELM SERIES ON INTERNATIONAL
ACCOUNTING AND FINANCE
Edited by C.W. Nobes

International Classification of Financial Reporting
Christopher Nobes

International Accounting: A Survey
J.M. Samuals and A.G. Piper

Accountants' Liability in the 1980s

An International View

EDITED BY E.P. MINNIS AND C.W. NOBES

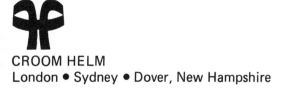

CROOM HELM
London • Sydney • Dover, New Hampshire

© 1985 E.P. Minnis and C.W. Nobes
Croom Helm Ltd, Provident House, Burrell Row,
Beckenham, Kent BR3 1AT

Croom Helm Australia Pty Ltd, Suite 4, 6th Floor,
64-76 Kippax Street, Surry Hills, NSW 2010, Australia

British Library Cataloguing in Publication Data

Accountants' liability in the 1980s: an
    international view.
    1. Accountants—Malpractice—Great Britain
    2. Negligence—Great Britain 3. Liability
    (Law)—Great Britain 4. Accountants—
    Malpractice—United States. 5. Negligence—
    United States 6. Liability (Law)—United States
    I. Minnis, E.P. II. Nobes, C.W.
    344.1063'2   KD2974

    ISBN 0-7099-1830-5

Croom Helm, 51 Washington Street, Dover,
New Hampshire 03820, USA

Library of Congress Cataloging in Publication Data
Main entry under title:

Accountants' liability in the 1980s.

    Bibliography:p.
    1. Accountants—Malpractice—Great Britain.
2. Accountants—Malpractice—United States.
I. Minnis, E.P., 1924—   II. Nobes, Christopher.
K4375.A22A27   1985   346.03'3   85—14960
ISBN 0-7099-1830-5   342.633

Printed and bound in Great Britain by
Biddles Ltd, Guildford and King's Lynn

Contents

PREFACE

This book is a joint effort of those involved in a conference on accountants' professional liability held at the University of Strathclyde on May 24, 1984. We were greatly assisted in the planning and organisation of the conference by Bill Morrison of KMG Thomson McLintock, a visiting professor at Strathclyde. We also acknowledge the help of Richard Blackburn of Touche Ross.

In compiling this book, we have received excellent co-operation from the four main speakers at the conference. Many useful comments on our material have also been provided by Janet Debman of Arthur Young, Tommy Docherty of Glasgow College, Tom Lee of Edinburgh University and Ian Lloyd of Strathclyde University Law School. Susanne Robertson has coped admirably with the intricacies of word-processed photo-reproduction.

NOTES ON CONTRIBUTORS

Editors :   E P Minnis is senior lecturer in
              accountancy at the University of
              Strathclyde.

              C W Nobes is Professor of
              Accounting at the University of
              Strathclyde.

Speakers :   W D Prosser, QC, is Dean of the
              Faculty of Advocates, Edinburgh.

              P S Christie is Director of the
              Professional Indemnity Division of
              J H Minet and Co, Canada.

              R`H Murray is General Counsel to
              Touche Ross & Co, New York and to
              Touche Ross International.

              P J Rutteman, CBE, is National
              Technical Partner, Arthur Young,
              UK.

PART I

BACKGROUND AND SUMMARY

Chapter One

ACCOUNTANTS' PROFESSIONAL LIABILITY UP TO HEDLEY BYRNE

E P Minnis

"Unless we confine the operation of such contracts as this (where every passerby who was injured can sue) to the parties who enter into them, the most absurd and outrageous consequences to which I can see no limit would ensue."   Abinger L J (1842)[1]

The existence of professional liability rests upon a recognisable and determinable standard of performance; in this case, the duty of care by an accountant to another party, who has the right of recovery of damages if he suffers injury from a breach of the duty.   The determination of who can recover damages has been a matter of much legal debate, centring around such issues as privity, the nature of loss, and the nature of third parties.   An action for damages against an accountant is likely to succeed only where :

(i)   A owes a duty of care to B;
(ii)   A has failed in that duty because of his poor performance;
(iii) B has suffered a measurable loss as a result of A's breach of duty.

The courts may endeavour to compensate B by the award of damages that put him in the same position he would have been in, but for A's breach of duty; for example, by awarding damages to B equal to the loss incurred as a result of A's negligence. There are many very difficult questions here; which the courts have been seeking to answer for a

3

long time.   For example:

(a)   How do we determine the duty that is owed?
(b)   How do we determine the persons or the classes of persons to whom the duty is owed?
(c)   How do we determine the nature and extent of the damage suffered - physical, economic, financial?
(d)   How do we determine what damage is to be recompensed, and what is not to be recompensed?
(e)   What are the rights of third parties?

Throughout the history of contract law, there had to be privity of contract between parties before an action in negligence could be brought. Failing this, the action had to be based either on fraud or deceit.   In <u>Winterbottom v Wright</u> (1842)[2] the plaintiff was denied the right to recover damages because of the absence of privity of contract, notwithstanding the physical injury of the plaintiff.[3]

Damages for physical injuries were awarded earlier in the USA than in the UK.   In <u>Thomas v Winchester</u> (1852), the right of recovery was granted to a third party where physical injury was suffered as a result of the inproper labelling of drugs.   It was held that one had a duty to avoid actions that were likely to endanger the lives of others.   The principle was extended even further in the USA in 1916, to the use of articles which are not dangerous in themselves but which might become a danger to life and limb through negligence in·their manufacture.   In <u>MacPherson v Buick Motor Company</u> (1916)[4] a third party was granted the right of recovery because of physical injury resulting from the negligent manufacture of a car.

In the UK, the courts, though anxious to give compensation where it was due, have been reluctant to extend the boundaries of liability too easily. The case of <u>Derry v Peek</u> (1889)[5] posed the question of financial loss suffered by a third party where there was no fiduciary or contractual relationship.   The action could not be brought in

4

negligence, and so had to be brought in deceit. It was then easy to show that the defendant accountant's report, though negligently prepared was not fraudulently made. There was no deceit, and so the action failed. The precedent in this case was followed in the case of <u>Le Lievre v Gould</u> (1893)[6] where the plaintiff had suffered a financial loss as a result of certificates that were negligently and incorrectly drawn by the defendant, a surveyor. The defendant was employed and paid by a third party. Lord Justice Bowden pointed out that the law does not consider that what a man writes on paper is like a gun or other dangerous instrument. In the absence of contract the law does not hold him responsible for producing his certificate carelessly : "... a man is entitled to be as negligent as he pleases towards the whole world if he owed no duty to them" (Lord Esher). Hence we see that negligence alone did not create a liability for damages; a duty of care had also to be proved.

Professional accountants were not alone in trying to resolve the problem of professional liability. Many cases are documented relating to other professions, e.g. doctors, lawyers and surveyors. Indeed the legal profession preceded the accountancy profession in recognising the right of recovery of damages for financial loss suffered by a party to a contract.[7] They also preceded the change in the USA where this right was denied to a claimant in 1919.[8]

In the USA the restraints against an action to recover financial loss and against an action by a third party were removed at the same time, in the case of <u>Glanzer v Shepard</u> (1922).[9] In this case, the plaintiff was allowed to bring an action in negligence for the recovery of a financial loss suffered as a result of the negligence of the defendant, with whom he had no contractual relationship. Judge Cardozo stated that the plaintiff was allowed to bring this action in negligence because of :

(i) Duty.
Duty arising out of contract normally had to

be established.   In this case, since the
certificate was all important to the parties
involved, the court must impose a duty.

(ii) Proximity and Class.
The third party, the plaintiff, was known to
the main parties to the contract before their
contract was sealed.   Indeed the doctrine of
the foreseen third party could easily be
invoked - a party so close as to imply a
contractual relationship.

It is interesting to note that Judge Cardozo
is here extending the boundaries of liability.
Compare this with his anxieties as expressed in
the Ultramares case (1931).[10]   Here the
defendants (accountants) had been employed by J
Stern & Co to prepare and report on a balance
sheet that showed its financial position.   The
accountants knew that these statements were used
by Stern & Co to help them raise finance.   The
accountants gave Stern & Co thirty-two copies of
their statement.   Ultramares Corporation, on the
strength of one of these statements, invested in
Stern & Co.   The statement was subsequently found
to be negligently and incorrectly prepared.
Ultramares lost the funds so invested and sued in
common law for deceit and negligence.   The court
dismissed the action since, in the absence of a
contractual relationship, the accountants owed no
duty of care to the plaintiff.[11]   Note, however,
that Cardozo showed much concern for the injured
third party. He considered whether the
accountant's balance sheet and report were drawn
so negligently as to suggest that the accountant
might not himself have believed in their accuracy:
whether they were prepared with reckless disregard
for the truth.   If so, this might have supported
a charge of gross negligence, which is equivalent
to constructive fraud.   If this was so, then the
absence of privity of contract would not have been
a bar to an action by a third party for the
recovery of damages for negligence.
This case, heard within ten years of Glanzer
v Shepard,[12] finds Judge Cardozo taking what might

appear to be a quite different stance. The main facts in the two cases are somewhat similar, the defendants being recognised experts in their chosen fields, preparing reports which they knew would be used to induce a third party to make a financial investment, the third party being known to the defendants. The plaintiffs, in both cases, acting on the strength of the negligently prepared reports, invested funds which they subsequently lost. In the Glanzer case, as mentioned above, Judge Cardozo had regard to the importance of the report and the foreseen third party. Yet in the Ultramares case he made an impassioned plea against the possibly uncontrolled expansion of the boundaries of accountants' professional liability. In the Glanzer case, the certificate could be used only by the plaintiff. In the Ultramares case, publication of the accounting report exposed the accountant to a limitless number of claims. Such an extension of liability could have constituted a dangerous social precedent, threatening the very survival of the fledgling accountancy profession of the 1930s. Judge Cardozo was aware of all this.[13]

In the non-accounting, Scottish case of <u>Donoghue v Stevenson</u>,[14] an injured third party was allowed to recover damages. The facts in this case were that the plaintiff became ill after finding a snail in her drink. The drink had been bought for her; so she had no contract with either the vendor or the manufacturer. She therefore brought an action in deceit against the manufacturer. The House of Lords upheld her contention that the manufacturer owed a duty to the ultimate consumer of his product.

<u>Donoghue v Stevenson</u> is particularly famous for Lord Atkin's celebrated "neighbourhood test". Stated briefly, he said that the rule of love thy neighbour becomes in law, "do not injure him". And in answer to the question, who is my neighbour, the answer is anyone who can be injured as a result of my actions - so that I should have foreseen this.

In spite of the decision by the House of Lords in the above case, the Courts were still reluctant to recognise a right of recovery for a third party who had suffered financial loss. In _Candler v Crane Christmas & Co_ (1951),[15]the defendants (a firm of accountants) prepared a set of accounts for a tin-mining company, knowing that they were to be used to induce the plaintiff to invest in the company. The draft accounts were shown to the plaintiff in the presence of the audit clerk who prepared them. The accounts were prepared negligently - though not fraudulently. They did not portray a true and fair view of the position of the company. The plaintiff invested in the company and lost his investment. He brought an action for negligence against the accountants.

The judge found that, even though the accounts were prepared negligently, but without fraud or deceit, in the absence of a contractual or fiduciary relationship, there was no duty owed by the defendant to the plaintiff, a third party. The case was dismissed and, on appeal, the Court of Appeal upheld the decision on a majority vote. Lord Denning, in his dissenting judgement expressed the view that the law would fail to serve the best interests of the community if it should hold that accountants and auditors owe a duty to no-one but their clients.

Lords Cohen and Asquith, who delivered the majority verdict, based their decision very largely on _Le Lievre v Gould_.[16] Lord Denning could not agree with this because he felt that the decision in that case had two serious errors : (i) it allowed only contracting parties to sue, and (ii) in the absence of a contractual relationship, there was no remedy in negligence for a third party, even though the offending statement was meant for his use, he did use it and suffered a loss as a result. Nor could Denning accept the distinction being made between physical damage and financial damage. Admittedly, in some cases involving financial loss, proximity might be insufficient to give rise to a duty of care. But once that duty is established, he could not see how the liability must then depend on the nature of the damage. Note that Lord Denning was not

calling for the unlimited extension of the
boundaries of accountants' liability. He was at
pains to emphasise that liability should not be
extended to absolute strangers, or those to whom
his employer or client might show the statement
without his knowledge or consent.

The comfort derived by accountants from the
Candler case was removed by the decision of the
House of Lords in <u>Hedley Byrne and Co Ltd v Heller
and Partners Ltd</u> (1964).[17] This case did not
concern accountants but banks. Briefly, the
facts were that A, the plaintiff, asked its
bankers, B, to investigate a client, C, for whom A
had placed large forward advertising orders. B
asked the client's bank, D, for information in
confidence about the financial standing of C. D
provided B with a certificate of credit-worthiness
on C with a disclaimer of responsibility. B
passed this on to A. At the time the certificate
was given, C was in financial difficulty and was
heavily in debt to D. On the strength of the
certificate the plaintiff, A, allowed its
contracts with C to stand. C went into
liquidation and A was unable to recover its
outlays. A therefore brought an action against D
for damages resulting from D's negligent
misrepresentations in their certificate.

The case eventually went to the House of
Lords where there was a unanimous decision that
the plaintiffs could not recover damages - because
the defendants had placed a disclaimer of
responsibility on their certificate. But there
were two other aspects of this case that were far
more important to accountants than the actual
decision :

(i) The views expressed by their Lordships on the
circumstances in which negligent but honest
misrepresentations could give rise to an
action in damages, in the absence of a
contractual relationship, and

(ii) The observation of their Lordships that the
Candler case was wrongly decided and that
they would have agreed with the dissenting

judgement of Lord Denning.

Their Lordships recognised that justice demanded that one who suffered economic or financial loss as a result of the negligence of another should have a right of recovery against that other, even in the absence of a contractual or fiduciary relationship between them. Their Lordships also realised that allowing justice to the claimants might at the same time create an unjust and inequitable situation for the defendant because of the enormity of the number of claims that might arise, and the increasing lack of proximity of the claimants to the defendant. They therefore sought a means of providing justice to the one and not at the same time creating injustice to the other.

While agreeing with Lord Denning in the Candler case, they wanted a test that would establish whether a duty of care is owed, a test that was more specific and restrictive than Denning's. They therefore turned to Lord Atkin's test in <u>Donoghue v Stevenson</u>. The general opinion of their Lordships seemed to be that, where A is in such a position that his advice might reasonably be expected to be relied upon by others, then a duty of care will arise. If A can be said to have assumed responsibility for the information and advice then, through the doctrine of assumpsit, he might incur liability for any economic or financial loss accruing to another as a result of relying on him. The case is said to be calling for a "special relationship" between the parties - where, but for the absence of consideration, there would have been a contract between them.

Even though avoiding Cardozo's indeterminate liability, their Lordships were by no means unanimous or clear on the exact boundary of liability. This case has been regarded subsequently as supplying an appropriate test for determining the existence of a duty of care. But the determination of the boundary has been the subject of much debate and obiter dicta in subsequent cases in the UK and Commonwealth.

Notes

(1) Abinger, L J, in <u>Winterbottom v Wright</u> (1842)
     10 M & N 109.
(2) Ibid.
(3) Damages were awarded for physical injury in a
     later case, <u>Heaven v Pender</u> (1883) 11 QB 503.
(4) 217 NY 382 111 NE 1050.
(5) 14 App Cas 337. For an action of deceit to
     succeed, the plaintiff must prove that the
     defendant's statement or representation was
     made knowing that it was false; or without
     belief in its truth; or with reckless
     disregard for the truth. The proof of any
     of these is difficult in relation to
     accounting statements since he would have to
     prove more than that the accountant acted
     without reasonable care but also that he was
     aware of the shortcomings of his statement.
(6) <u>Le Lievre v Gould</u> (1893), 1 QB 491, 9 TLR
     243, CA.
(7) In 1914 a mortgager claimed against his
     solicitor on the grounds that he had suffered
     a financial loss because he had been wrongly
     advised by the solicitor. It was held that
     there was a breach of duty, arising out of
     the fiduciary relationship between them.
     (<u>Nocton v Lord Ashburton</u> (1914) AC 932.)
(8) In the US case of <u>Landell v Lybrand</u> (264 Pa
     406, 107 A 763, 1919), the plaintiff, who
     suffered financial loss as a result of the
     alleged careless audit and subsequent
     misrepresentations of an accountant, was not
     allowed to bring an action in negligence, and
     had to resort to an action based on fraud and
     deceit - neither of which could be proved.
(9) 233 NY 236, 135 NE 275.
(10) <u>Ultramares Corporation v Touche et al</u> 255 NY
     170, 174 NE 441.
(11) Cardozo C J gave his now famous warning of
     leaving auditors liable for a thoughtless
     slip or blunder or the failure to detect
     theft or forgery which might expose them to
     claims for an indeterminate amount, for an
     indeterminate time, to an indeterminate

class.

(12) As note 9.

(13) Compare this situation of the 1930s with that
of 1968 as portrayed in the case of <u>Rusch
Factors v Levin</u>, 284 F Supp 85 (1968).   In
this case, the court considered whether an
innocent party should bear losses rather than
their being borne by a negligent accountant
who is able to be protected by insurance, the
cost of which can be passed on.

(14) AC 562.

(15) 2 KB 164.

(16) As note 6.

(17) <u>Hedley Byrne & Co v Heller & Partners Ltd</u>,
1964, AC 465.

Chapter Two

PROFESSIONAL LIABILITY AFTER HEDLEY BYRNE

E P Minnis

"It seems fairly clear that society, as represented by the press and politicians, will continue to expect more of professions generally in order that they (the professions) justify their position in society".   Alan Davison[1]

It is an understatement to say that the North American scene as portrayed by Rick Murray and Peter Christie is frightening.   Fortunately for accountants and auditors in the UK, the courts here demonstrate a greater concern for equity. Thus, while accepting that accountants must take some responsibility for negligent acts, the courts have been concerned to control the extension of any liability arising from these acts.   The courts have always been mindful of Cardozo's warning,[2] as was shown in the speeches of each of the Law Lords in the Hedley Byrne case.[3] Thereafter, cases in Britain and the Commonwealth demonstrate this search for fairness to both sides.   There is the recognition that a professional can owe a duty of care to a third party in the absence of a contractual or fiduciary relationship;   a recognition that a professional can incur liability to a third party for economic or financial loss;   but with an equal recognition that a professional whose report can easily be distributed far and wide might incur unlimited liability.   There is, therefore, a need to restrain the uncontrolled expansion of this liability.   Many Commonwealth cases as well as UK ases are worthy of study in order to understand how accountants' liability has developed since Hedley Byrne.

Developments in the Commonwealth

In New Zealand, the decision in <u>Diamond Manufacturing Co Ltd v Hamilton (1968)</u>[4] was arrived at after a detailed consideration of Hedley Byrne. The facts were very similar to those in the Candler case. The defendant, D, had prepared accounts and showed them to P who, relying on them, made an investment. P subsequently suffered a financial loss on his investment and sued D for negligence. In the first court it was held that D was not liable since the accounts were not prepared for the sole purpose of investment negotiations. This decision was reversed by the appeal court because it was held that a special relationship of the Hedley Byrne type existed between the parties.

The Australian case of <u>MLC Assurance Co Ltd v Evatt (1971)</u>[5] went to the Privy Council. It concerned an Insurance company, D, which gave gratuitous advice to a client, P, who made an investment on the basis of this advice, and suffered a financial loss because the advice was wrong. P brought an action against D based on the principle of special relationship, as established in Hedley Byrne. The majority decision of the Privy Council was that, since the giving of this type of advice was not the main business of the insurance company which professed no special expertise in this field, the company incurred no liability. It owed a duty to be honest, but not a duty to be careful.

In <u>Haig v Bamford (1977)</u>,[6] a Canadian case, the criteria for determining the existence of a duty of care to a third party were discussed at some length. In this case S agreed to make a loan to B, provided that:

    (i)   satisfactorily audited accounts were produced, and

    (ii) additional capital of $20,000 could be raised.

S asked D to prepare the required statement, and informed him that he was seeking additional finance. When the statement was produced, S's manager showed it to P, who relied on it when investing $22,500 in the company. P subsequently lost his investment and brought an action against D. Note that, unlike the Candler case, D did not have P in mind as an individual, nor know him, nor show him the accounts. D maintained that his engagement was not an audit, and therefore that he owed no duty of care to P. In order to determine whether D was liable to P one must decide :

      (i)   whether it is enough to know that the statement would be relied on by a particular class, and

      (ii) whether P was a member of that class.

The Supreme Court held that the answer to both these questions was "yes"; that the engagement was an audit; that D's report was in the form of an audit report; and that D was guilty of serious dereliction of duty. It was pointed out that several tests might be used to determine whether or not a duty of care is owed, including (a) foreseeability and reliance, (b) knowledge of a class, and (c) knowledge of the individual. The foreseeability test was expressly ignored in this case, as it was never contended that D had any prior knowledge of P. Here, knowledge of a class was the more appropriate test of a duty of care. D was told by S that he was looking for additional finance, so he must have contemplated that his accounts might have been relied upon and used by financiers. It was also pointed out in this case that accountants must now move away from the protective umbrella provided by Cardozo in the Ultramares case;[7] that accountants now have a considerable prestige in society and so they must be prepared to accept a commensurate increase in responsibility to society.

Scott Group Ltd v McFarlane (1975),[8] a New Zealand case, is particularly interesting for the learned discussion of many of the doctrines established in the effort to control the expansion of professional liability, following Hedley Byrne, and in particular for the discussion of reasonable foreseeability. The facts in the case are fairly straightforward. P, relying on the audited group accounts of J D H Ltd, made a successful take-over bid for the company. The audited accounts, which were not qualified, contained several material errors. P claimed that the purchase price that he paid was excessive due to the accounting errors that had since come to light. P therefore raised an action to recover damages from the auditor, D; the amount claimed being the excess of the price he paid for the shares over the value of the shares at time of purchase. P maintained that D ought reasonably to have foreseen that the accounts were likely to be relied on by him as an intending purchaser of the company and therefore owed him a duty of care.

In the lower court it was established that, at the time of the audit, the accountants had no knowledge of any likely take-over bid for the company. In these circumstances it was held that no special relationship could exist between the plaintiff and the defendant, and the latter could not be said to owe a duty of care to the former. In the Court of Appeal the plaintiff's case was dismissed on a majority vote :

Richmond P held that no duty of care was owed, and so P could not succeed.

Cooke J also held that P could not succeed, but for a different reason than that given by Richmond P. Cooke J held that even though a duty of care was owed by D to P, P could not recover because he had not proved his loss.

Woodhouse J held that D did owe a duty of care to P and so P should have recovered damages.

Richmond P, in finding that no duty of care was owed, did not follow the doctrine of foreseeability but preferred to base his findings on the test established for negligent misstatements. This assumes that the maker of the statement has assumed responsibility for his statement, and that he recognises that he would owe a duty of care to a particular class of persons who might rely on it.   Richmond P felt that, only if we can say that the maker of the statement must have had a person or class of persons specially in mind (i.e. if he voluntarily undertakes a duty of care), can we say that a duty of care is owed.   He considered that, today, many different classes of persons might use and rely on statements prepared by accountants, shareholders, investors and others.   This could result in an excessive extension of the boundaries of liability for the accountant.   He felt that it would be wrong to give the accountant such an extensive responsibility, which goes beyond that special relationship envisaged in Hedley Byrne.

Cooke J, basing his findings on the doctrine of foreseeability, held that a duty of care was owed by D to P.   The excessive purchase price paid, though showing that the audit had a causative effect, did not provide a basis on which damages should be assessed.   For this, Cooke preferred to turn to the principle established in deceit cases :   determining the difference between the price paid and the actual value at time of purchase.   In this case, the value of the assets at time of purchase was considerably in excess of the price paid (which was relatively small). Hence the plaintiff had not really suffered a loss, since this excess was greater than the provision that a prudent accountant would have made.   He held, therefore, that P was not entitled to recover any damages.   Woodhouse J felt that accountants ought to accept a greater responsibility than that envisaged by Cardozo C J in the Ultramares case nearly 50 years previously. He preferred to base his findings on Wilberforce's neighbourhood doctrine developed in <u>Anns v Merton London Borough Council</u>.[9] Following the two-stage test developed in that case, he found that :

(i)   when auditors report on a public company they must be taken to have accepted a responsibility to a wider group than that company's shareholders, including those persons whom they ought reasonably

to have foreseen might have to rely on
the accounts in their dealings with the
company. In his opinion, therefore,
there was a sufficient relationship of
proximity in this case.

(ii) He could find no circumstances in this
case that might mitigate the resulting
liability, and so he would have awarded
the appellants the full damages claimed.

Liability in Other Professions

Considerable advances have been made in the
law relating to professional negligence through
cases involving other professions, e.g.
solicitors. In <u>Groom v Crocker</u>[10] it was held
that a solicitor owed no duty of care to his
client beyond the contractual duties arising from
his retainer. This remained the accepted
principle until challenged by Lord Denning as
Master of the Rolls in <u>Esso Petroleum Co Ltd v
Mardon (1976)</u>.[11] This view was confirmed by the
decision in the Midland Bank case,[12] where it was
held that a solicitor was liable in negligence for
failing to register an option. It was also held
that <u>Groom v Crocker</u> was inconsistent with Hedley
Byrne and that it was no longer good law.

In the Allied Finance case (1980),[13] a
solicitor whose actions came near to being
fraudulent escaped a charge of damages because it
was held that only in exceptional circumstances
could a solicitor owe a duty of care to the other
party with whom his client has a contract. His
job is to look after his client's interest, not
other people's, in a way that might be detrimental
to his client.

<u>Ross v Caunters</u> (1980)[14] raised another
problem relating to solicitors. That is, the
extent of the duty of care owed by a solicitor to
a third party who is to benefit by work he does on
the instruction of his client. It was held that
a solicitor can be liable in tort to someone who
is not his client; that a solicitor, acting for
the benefit of another on the instructions of his
client, owes a duty of care to that other.

It is obvious from these cases that the problem facing the courts in relation to solicitors is very similar to that in relation to accountants : how to define the ambit of the solicitor's duty of care while at the same time remembering that the recognition of a duty to the parties could create an unacceptable conflict with the primary duty owed to the solicitor's client.

Recent UK Developments

In Britain, Hedley Byrne[15] seemed to settle the position of the auditor with respect to liability to third parties for negligence. The third party should be known, and known to be relying on the accounting statement. There had to be a special relationship. Two cases in particular changed these principles, <u>Jeb Fasteners v Marks Bloom & Co</u> (1981)[16] and <u>Twomax Ltd v Dickson McFarlane & Robinson (1983)</u>.[17]

In the Jeb Fasteners case, the plaintiff brought an action for negligence against D, claiming that he had made a successful take-over bid for a company, relying on that company's accounts which were prepared by D. He did not contend that D knew that he would rely on the accounts. The accounts were negligently prepared; for example, stocks were wrongly described in the balance sheet. It was subsequently revealed that P knew about the over-valuation of stocks before his bid became final. The action failed because Woolf J concluded that :

    (i)   the take-over was really aimed at acquiring the services of two directors of the company, and that

    (ii) P would have acquired the company, no matter what profits were showing.

Woolf J also found that :

    (a)   D owed a duty of care to P based on the doctrine of foreseeability or reasonable reliance; and

    (b)   it is more difficult to prove causation of loss than to prove duty of care.

In Hedley Byrne their Lordships had required

proof of a "special relationship" before a duty of care could be said to be owed. Subsequent cases relied on this theory where it was assumed that the defendant either knew or ought to have known that the plaintiff would rely on the accounts and would suffer damage if the accounts were negligently prepared. In the Candler case[18] Lord Denning's test was stricter than that in Hedley Byrne. He felt that a duty of care was only owed to those to whom the defendant himself showed the accounts, or those to whom his employer showed the accounts with his consent. But Lord Denning did not think that a duty of care could be owed to absolute strangers. Woolf J had no doubt that, in this case (Jeb Fasteners), D did owe a duty of care to P because, when the accounts were prepared, D had knowledge of P or should have had him in his contemplation. Woolf based his judgement on Wilberforce's two-stage reasoning in the Anns case.[19]

Lest he should create an indeterminate liability, however, Woolf J insisted on a reasonable reliance test in determining whether or not a duty was owed :

> If the situation is one where it would not be reasonable for the accounts to be relied on, then, in the absence of express knowledge, the auditor would be under no duty. This places a limit on the circumstances in which the audited accounts can be relied on and the period for which they can be relied on. The longer the period which elapses prior to the accounts being relied on, from the date on which the auditor gave his certificate, the more difficult it will be to establish that the auditor ought to have foreseen that his certificate would, in those circumstances, be relied on. (3 All ER, 296.)

The problem of the unrestricted time period referred to here by Mr Justice Woolfe has never been properly resolved and only recently has a proposal been made that goes some way to correcting it. The question is, if an accountant prepares his report negligently, what is the maximum time period between the preparation and the damage that would still enable a successful action for recovery of damages. The risk of actions for damages on work done in a long-gone era has been a bane in the life of many retired accountants. Such risks make comprehensive insurance most expensive and very difficult to obtain. The Law Reform Committee of the House of Commons has recently examined this area and, in its report entitled <u>Latent Damages</u>, it recommended that the existing six year period of limitation should be subject to an extension which would allow a plaintiff three years from the date when significant damage was discovered but up to 15 years from the original breach of duty. This matter has not been fully discussed yet by the Scottish Law Commission.

One of the most recent cases relating to accountants' professional negligence is that of <u>Twomax Ltd & Ors v Dickson, MacFarlane & Robinson</u>.[20] The case related to an action for damages brought by three persons against a firm of accountants because of the negligent audit of a company. The audited accounts for the years prior to 1975 were said to be most misleading. The results shown were as follows :

     Year to 31 March 1971, £32,880 loss
     Year to 31 March 1972, £12,318 loss
     Year to 31 March 1973, £20,346 profit

Thus it appeared that the company had made a remarkable recovery in three years, from a loss of £32,880 to a profit of £20,346, making it a very good investment prospect. Twomax Ltd therefore invested heavily in this company, a part of its investment being the purchase of the shareholding of one of the company's directors. By 1975 however it became obvious that things were not going as well as they might and so another accountant was called in to carry out an investigation. Following this investigation, the company went into receivership in 1975 and then into liquidation. Twomax Ltd lost its entire investment.

The action related to the audits for the years 1972 and 1973 in particular, and also to

1975.   In fact, what looked like a wonderful recovery between 1971 and 1973 turned into a loss of £87,727 by 1975.   The audits were said to be negligently performed in several respects.   For example, it was averred that the auditors failed to make any check on the company's system of stock control or on the basis of valuation of stock. The stock figures shown in the accounts were felt to be seriously inaccurate, although this could not be proved.   The only concrete errors established in the 1973 accounts in relation to the profit figure were the understatement of doubtful debts by £357 and errors in agents' commission of £3200.   Thus £3567 was to be deducted from the trading profit shown as £20346, reducing it to £16779.   What the true profit or loss for that year ought to have been was never proved.   However this did not prevent Lord Stewart from holding thus :

> Nevertheless I am satisfied that the pursuers have established their averment that the accounts of Kintyre upon which they relied were grossly misleading and produced a seriously distorted picture of the company's affairs.

Lord Stewart felt that the main task was to decide whether the defendants owed a duty of care to the plaintiffs.   If one were to follow the neighbourhood or proximity principle as laid down in <u>Donoghue v Stevenson</u>[21] the answer would be "yes".   If one were to follow the principles laid down in Hedley Byrne, where limitations were placed on the extension of liability brought about by applying the neighbour principle, then he felt that the answer would be "no".   He drew attention to the fact that, in Hedley Byrne, their Lordships saw the need to prove a special relationship - a relationship that can be seen as giving rise to a special duty to use care in making a statement :

> The question in any given case is whether the nature of the relationship is such that one party can fairly be held to have assumed a responsibility to the other as regards the reliability of the advice or information.   I do not think that such a relationship should

be found to exist unless, at least, the maker of the statement was, or ought to have been, aware that his advice or information would in fact be made available to and be relied on by a particular person or class of persons for the purposes of a particular transaction or type of transaction.

Among the other cases considered by Lord Stewart were <u>Ross v Caunters</u> and <u>Jeb Fasteners Ltd v Marks Bloom & Co</u>. About the latter case, Lord Stewart said :

The approach of Woolf J commends itself to me. If I may respectfully say so, it appears to combine the simplicity of the proximity or neighbour principle with a limitation which has regard to the warning against exposing accountants 'to a liability in an indeterminate amount for an indeterminate time to an indeterminate class' ... and also to Lord Wilberforce's second question in the passage already quoted from Anns.[22]

He then went on to point out that, at the time of the audits, the auditor had no knowledge of the plaintiffs, but he did know that :

(i)   the company was in serious financial difficulties,

(ii)   one of the directors wanted to sell his holding, which was substantial,

(iii) accounts were being made available to lenders, and

(iv) unqualified audit certificates gave comfort to potential lenders.

Lord Stewart therefore concluded that the auditor must have foreseen that the accounts would be relied on by an investor. Following Wilberforce's test in Anns case, he held that :

(i)   the auditor did owe a duty of care to the plaintiffs, and

(ii)   he could see no circumstances that would justify a mitigation of liability.

The Jeb Fasteners case established the principle that the auditor might be liable to a

third party if "reasonable foreseeability" has
been proved.   This principle was later applied in
the Twomax case, thereby confirming its place in
the laws of the UK.

Looking Ahead

Considering many of the cases discussed by
Peter Christie and Rick Murray, for example, the
Panzirer case[23] or the Saxon Industries debacle,
it seems fair to say that accountants in North
America are facing "... a liability in an
indeterminate amount for an indeterminate time to
an indeterminate class".   Following the constant
increases in size and number of payments having to
be made by insurance companies on behalf of
accountants (one of the Big Eight firms recently
made an out of court settlement of $49m, followed
a few weeks later by another firm's out of court
settlement of $23m),[24] indemnity costs including
general premiums and premiums for excess coverage
are expected to rise sharply in the USA in 1985.
In Britain the boundaries of accountants'
professional liability are being constantly
expanded, but at a slower pace.   Here, too,
claims against accountants are increasing in both
size and number.[25]   There are many reasons why
accountants and auditors are becoming more
susceptible to negligence suits;   for example :

    (i)   they are being required more and more
            to report on matters that rely on their
            personal opinion, which can be more
            easily challenged;

    (ii)   they are engaging in more non-audit
            engagements, which more easily give
            rise to litigation;

    (iii) the requirements of several accounting
            and auditing standards, statutory
            regulations, etc, have increased the
            risk of litigation;

    (iv) the confusion of understanding about
            the real duty of an auditor - the
            expectation gap - often gives rise to
            litigation.

As our speakers said, there is a real risk that the profession might be driven into a defensive attitude, rather than an active one, which is so necessary for a constantly developing profession. There is already much evidence of the growth of this protective attitude as may be seen in some professional pronouncements and in the non-committal manner in which many reports are written. The English Institute took counsel's opinion following the decision in the Hedley Byrne case and thereafter issued a very confident statement suggesting that accountants were not likely to incur liability for negligence to third parties who had suffered only financial loss, except in very limited circumstances. In the light of subsequent cases this opinion has had to be changed. Recent pronouncements and guidelines demonstrate less confidence against the risk of litigation and many stress ways of avoiding it. In 1983 the Institute of Chartered Accountants in England and Wales felt bound to issue some guidance to members. The statement first defined negligence, then discussed several acceptable defences to such a charge. This was followed by a description of several ways of minimising the risk of a charge of negligence in engagements where the accountant's responsibility was not determined by statute :

    (i)   the use of engagement letters,
    (ii)   the use of exclusion clauses,
    (iii) extra care with the definition of responsibility in engagements based on limited information, or those calling for rapid or specialist work,
    (iv)   definition of liability to third parties, and
    (v)   the use of disclaimers to third parties.

Perhaps the difficulty of the problem of professional liability can be gauged from the fact that the guidance ends in a note reminding members of the Indemnity Insurance Scheme arranged by the Institute. This impression is reinforced by the Institute's recent recommendation to members that they should increase their indemnity insurance cover to three times their total annual fees, or thirty times their highest fee.

The guideline emphasises the need for an auditor to make certain that his client understands the true purpose of an audit - that the auditor will carry out such an examination of the books and accounts as would allow him to state whether the accounts show a true and fair view; and that such an opinion is no guarantee of long life for the company or freedom from fraud or error. There is, however, the implication that the audit will be so planned as to give reasonable assurance that material fraud and error will be found. These points are highlighted by the recent spectacular collapse of Johnson Matthey Bankers, within weeks of receiving an unqualified audit report from its auditors, and its equally spectacular rescue by the Bank of England.

The extent of the auditor's responsibility for the detection of fraud and error has varied over the years, from the earliest times when it was a primary objective, to a time not long ago when it became a secondary objective, with management assuming the main responsibility for the protection of company assets. Auditors were, however, never completely free of responsibility, and have always been susceptible to litigation in this area. Today, fraud is again becoming a burning issue following many recent celebrated cases here, in the USA, and elsewhere. Fraud is increasing in size and complexity, and many cases are computer related and with management involvement. As a result, many public bodies are carrying out studies into the nature of fraud and its detection.[26]

The advice offered by our British speakers on this growing problem for British accountants is worthy of our most serious consideration. Paul Rutteman suggests that perhaps the most obvious guidance is to make sure that you secure your own quality control. He sees the improvement in quality control in recent years as a direct by-product of the legal problems. But good quality control costs a phenomenal amount : "thus, litigation and quality control has to some extent led to defensive auditing". Despite all that has gone before, he does not see it as all bad news : "... the quality of the profession has risen rapidly over the last few years. I think we are recruiting the best people, and there is no better protection than quality people". We must remember Dean Prosser's warning that a professional should keep his mind on his true function and endeavour to achieve that, rather than constantly worrying about liability and strategems to avoid it : "Liability, I would suggest, is merely the dark side of fulfilling a proud and responsible function and being willing to answer for things one has undertaken to do". There is much truth in his suggestion that "... the widening exposure to claims of negligence is broadly correlative to a very proper broadening of function and performance, ... the increased exposure is not really to be deplored. It really ought to be accepted as the other side of one's increasing responsibilities; accepted and, if possible, insured against".

Notes

(1)   A.G. Davison, "Auditors' Liability to Third Parties for Negligence", Accounting and Business Research, Autumn 1982, p 257.

(2)   Ultramares Corporation v Touche et al, 255 NY 170, NE 441 (1931).

(3)   Hedley Byrne & Co Ltd v Heller & Partners Ltd, (1964) A C 465.

(4)   NZ LR 705.

(5)   AC 793.

(6)   72 DLR (3d)68.

(7)   As note 2.

(8)   1 NZ LR 553 (CA).

(9)   (1978) A C 728. In this case, Lord Wilberforce expressed the view that the determination of the existence of a duty of care has to be approached in two stages :
      (i)   between D and P, is there a relationship of sufficient proximity or neighbourhood that would make D aware of the fact that his carelessness might injure P, and
      (ii) if so, are there any circumstances that might mitigate any resulting liability to D?

(10) (1939) 1 KB 194.

(11) 1 QB 801.

(12) Midland Bank v Hett, Stubbs & Kemp, (1979) Ch 384.

(13) Allied Finance and Investment Ltd v Haddow and Co, (1980) 2 NZ LR 428.

(14) 1 Ch 297.

(15) As note 3.

(16) (1981) 3 ALL ER 289.

(17) From the opinion of Lord Stewart in the Outer House of the Court of Session, Edinburgh, 5 March 1982.

(18) Candler v Crane Christmas & Co, (1951) 2 KB 164.

(19) As note 9.

(20) As note 17.

(21) (1932) AC 562.

(22) As note 9.

(23) Zelda L Panzirer v Emanuel L Wolf et al, 663 F 2d 365.

(24) International Accounting Bulletin, November 1984. The auditors of several other corporations have faced huge negligence suits

recently, e.g. the auditors of :
Continental Illinois National Bank ...$200m
Financial Corporation of America $1bn
(25) In the UK, Barclay's Bank appointed a receiver for the Hill Group of property developers following a report by the accountants. The accountants are now facing negligence claims on the basis that their report was incorrect. Also, the British Government is seeking damages of nearly £250m in the US Courts from the auditors of the failed De Lorean sports car company. It is interesting to note that this suit is being brought in the US Courts, and that the Government is claiming punitive damages.
(26) Some of the bodies looking into fraud are :
(i)   The APC of the Scottish Institute.
(ii) A committee of the English Institute which is to be chaired by Mr Ian H Davison.
(iii) Arthur Young with the Police Federation.
(iv) The English Audit Commission - computer fraud in Local Authorities.
(v)   A Fraud Investigation Group established by Mr Nigel Lawson.
Prominent members of society have also been speaking out against the growth of fraud and asking that something be done. Mr Alex Fletcher has expressed the hope that a standard on fraud will soon be published by the profession.

Chapter Three

SUMMARY AND HIGHLIGHTS OF CHAPTERS FOUR TO SEVEN

C W Nobes

The Root of Liability

In the past, much litigation arose out of unclear terms of engagement. However, the profession has now generally become much more precise and standardised in its terms, so that the specific job an accountant is doing is normally clear. Now, increasingly, the problems arise from implied duties to the contracting party and, further, to third parties. The most obvious general duty is to exercise reasonable care and to observe the standards of a competent member of the profession. The third parties concerned are those who, with reasonable foresight, could have been expected to be affected. The _Jeb Fasteners_ and _Twomax_ cases have confirmed that the accountant should foresee that almost anyone may rely on any public document. Attempts to limit this by terms of contract will not generally work; and neither will limiting the addressees of an audit report to "the members" (see references to Unfair Contract Terms Act in the ICAEW Statement _Professional Liability of Accountants and Auditors_, November 1983).

As usual, the USA is ahead of us here. In the case of Mrs Zelda Panzirer, a firm of auditors was held liable for her loss on shares in United Artists, because she invested on the advice of a financial journalist who had read the relevant

ancial statements that had a clean audit
port. However, the auditors were seen as the
most "suable" party (see "deep-pocket" discussion
in the section on "US Experience", below).

Reasonable Care

Cases in other professions, such as medicine and
architecture, will give guidance as to what a
court would regard as good practice or reasonable
care. It has fortunately been held that not all
errors are negligent and, further, that two or
more differing professional opinions may
nevertheless be respectable. On the other hand,
a court has also held that it may be possible for
accepted standard practice not to be good enough,
which has moved us on from the Royal Mail case of
Rex v Kylsant and Morland (1931). On the matter
of judgement, in a case involving a broker, a
court held that professional advice could not be
expected always to lead to the avoidance of loss.
However, for accountants, there is the added
problem of the degree to which one should now be a
bloodhound as well as a watchdog. Reliance on
others is becoming more and more risky, and the
courts appear increasingly to be demanding that,
if a test could be carried out, it should be.
Even if a duty of care is held to exist to a
particular litigant, detailed recourse to the
facts and a challenge to any claim of causation
may prove to be a defence. For example, in Jeb
Fasteners the error was held not to have caused
the loss. Unfortunately, the Twomax case ran
dangerously close to viewing a set of accounts as
a guarantee of future performance. Thus, it is
beginning to be the case that accountants must be
prepared to make forecasts of any disasters and to
publish them. The failure of auditors to use the
going concern qualification has recently been
commented on.[1]

Standards

The gradual proliferation of precise rules in
accounting is like a two-edged sword. On one

side, detailed standards allow detailed defences by accountants that they were following their professional rules. On the other side, possibilities for much more specific claims of negligence arise. However, in the long run, it must be in the interests of the profession to try to raise its standards by stating them. Nevertheless, several problems may arise.

First, competent and imaginative leaders of the profession may find themselves dangerously out of line with standard practice. However, a recent architects' case (<u>Kelly v Edinburgh Corporation</u>) offers some hope here. The architects claimed that they ignored a British Standard because their practices were better. On appeal, the court agreed. One would probably need a very good reputation to be confident in such a situation.

Secondly, the question arises of superior in-house standards such as may be found in large firms. Certainly in the USA, compliance with profession-wide standards would not be good enough if a firm had failed to carry out its own standard procedures. Lastly, there are dangers that the general level of standards will stagnate because of the increasing risks attached to new developments. For example, one might be encouraged never to move beyond an historical cost system because of the less objective nature of the alternatives. This would probably not well serve the readers of financial statements.

Advisory Services

As the area of work of accountants expands, so does their exposure to liability. To what extent should an accountant consult a lawyer when giving advice that might be wrong on law? Increasingly, there is a danger that if you could have consulted a lawyer, a court will hold that you should have done. One possible development that may help here is the hiring of specialist lawyers, actuaries, etc by firms of accountants. The danger is that, when you have in-house experts, the courts will be even more likely to find that you should have consulted them.

Another example of dangers comes from such work as providing profit forecasts or cash flow projections. You can be certain that they will not be exactly right, and this gives rise to the potential for litigation. It may also be easier than it is in auditing to establish a link between the provision of a service and a subsequent loss.

Insurance

At present, the professional indemnity insurance market is small, but exceptionally competitive. There are dangers in this for the future, particularly because this type of insurance is complex for the insurers. First, compared to house or motor insurance, it is hard to understand the changes in claims experience from year to year. Secondly, the cost of any particular claim is more difficult to determine than in other fields of insurance : the insurer has to establish that the events took place, he has to wait for the case to be settled. The long-tailed nature of this insurance is extreme; some cases are still unsettled after 15 years. This makes it difficult to price the insurance correctly, and this (coupled with the very competitive market) could lead to failures of underwriters, rising prices and difficulty in finding cover.

Let us turn to a few points that a firm seeking insurance should check. First, what exactly does a policy for 1985 cover? It will cover you for claims that you begin to anticipate in 1985 and about which you notify your insurers; this includes of course the claims actually made against you in 1985 that were not anticipated before 1985. However, it will probably not cover the work of 1985. This is a particular problem for sole practitioners who retire. However, no other system would be practicable for the insurers: the tail is long enough already.

Secondly, of what exactly should the insurer be notified? The answer is everything that could give rise to a claim. This means that it will be sensible to over-inform rather than under-inform, and that good systems must be in operation throughout the firm to ensure that notification gets to the appropriate partner and then to the insurer. It is worth remembering that there are often **two** insurers, who should both be notified. Thirdly, it is important to have a policy that protects innocent partners from another partner's fraud. This, of course, raises the nightmare of a bad partner signing the firm's proposal form, and thereby invalidating it due to not 'disclosing his knowledge of potential problems in the firm.

Fourth, geographical restriction clauses should be checked. It is not safe to assume that you need no coverage in other countries. For example, a client may be borrowing money from the USA, and this entails a potential for US jurisdiction. Fifth, there is the question of the scope of work covered. One has to make certain that consultancy, taxation and other work are covered, where appropriate. Lastly, when working on an insurance contract, a firm should make sure that the contract remains the creature of the insurer and his advisers. Otherwise, when ambiguity arises later, it may be held that the accountancy firm was involved in the drafting of the contract which should therefore be construed against it.

There remains the question of how much insurance cover to take out. Unfortunately, there is no simple calculation. There is no direct relationship between the size of fees and the potential liability. In a US case, an auditing firm was sued for $50m by an insurance company which had put up completion bonds to that value for the small construction company that was the audit client. The loss bore no relation to the audit fee or even to the turnover or capitalisation of the client. It may be more useful to examine the worrying trends of the size of claims and then to extrapolate these for the five years that it will take for today's work to become a settled claim.

US Experience

Recent UK litigation experience is beginning to resemble that of the USA a few years ago. This suggests that it may be worthwhile to look at the current US position and ask if it contains predictions for the UK.

Contrary to popular UK opinion the current litigation problems in the USA do not stem mainly from class actions and contingent fees, but from financial institutions who have lost money. This is combined with the ascendancy of a consumerism that tries to protect the buyer, and with the notion of "the deep pocket" whereby a litigant sues the party deemed most prosperous rather than most guilty.

The scope of the duty of care has been mentioned above, and it has been taken furthest in the USA. There is also an increasing tendency to demand that auditors should have predicted financial disasters. Further, the regulatory environment has turned against the profession by the invention of punitive damage statutes; for example, the Racketeering Influenced and Corrupt Organizations (RICO) Act. This is a federal law of the mid-1970s designed to combat organised crime by imposing treble damages. The definition of organised crime was a problem for Congress, who decided that it should include two violations of federal law within ten years. It was not long before banks and their lawyers realised that RICO damages might be obtained by suing firms of accountants who had been found guilty of negligence or SEC violations.

As a result of these and other problems, US insurance premiums have multiplied and almost become catastrophe insurance. There is also much personal trauma and professional disruption associated with massive lawsuits. In a recent New York case (Saxon Industries) all 300 partners of an accounting firm were classed as defendants and had their personal assets put at the disposal of the court for execution if necessary.

Forthcoming UK Problems

It seems that UK statutes and courts are less likely to turn so savagely against accountants as those in the USA have. However, several problems are coming our way. First, there is a tendency for large cases to spill over from one country to another, because of the multinational nature of companies, audit firms and major lenders. Second, as mentioned above, the work of accountants is moving into the riskier areas of advice, forecasting and perhaps the inclusion of CCA notes in "true and fair" accounts.

Also, some EEC Directives are adding the need to report on valuations : the Second Directive (1980 Act), when non-cash consideration is given for plc shares; and the Third Directive, when there is a particular kind of merger (fusion) that involves a share exchange ratio. Lastly, if the Fifth Directive goes through, the statutory liability of auditors will become heavier, and the requirement to warn the company and its shareholders of financial dangers will become more explicit.

Long-Run Defences

Many relevant factors under this heading are discussed in the Institute's statement on professional liability. The particular points below are raised in the main chapters of this book.

One response to increasing litigation has been a growing emphasis on quality. The profession starts with excellent graduates, who are carefully trained and supervised; audit trails are demanded and followed exhaustively; and quality control reviews are carried out. Firms have also learned to look out for risky clients. If possible they are avoided; if existing clients become risky much more work is done on them : double-checking, cash flow projections, technical advice, and so on. This defensive auditing is very expensive for the client but is necessary to mitigate the high risks for firms.

Another defence must be to tackle the "expectation gap" between what the profession is reasonably capable of doing and what is expected of it by some members of the public and some lawyers.   In North America, courts have begun to view accountants as having a public trust that far transcends any client relationship.   The profession here will have continually to challenge such a possible interpretation of its role.

Also, the profession may have to change some of its own attitudes.   Accountants will have to abandon the assumption that they are not going to be sued.   This will make clear that a competent professional job is no longer sufficient : careful defensive measures must be taken to leave proof that all reasonable steps were taken.   One must assume that one's working papers will be examined : for what they do not contain and for what they do contain.   A note of suspicions that were not subsequently investigated may be as damning as the absence of a record of a routine test.   To be aware constantly of these problems may also reduce the trauma when the inevitable case comes along.

The profession must also abandon reliance on clients' representations or even on third party confirmations, particularly where there were initial suspicions.   Partners may also have to increase supervision of audit staff and to ensure that there are good upward channels of communication for suspicions.   The famous McKessan and Robbins case might have never happened if a junior member of an audit team had recognised that goods cannot be moved from Australia to San Francisco by lorry.

PART II

CONFERENCE ADDRESSES

Chapter Four

THE LEGAL POSITION IN THE UK

W D Prosser, QC[*]

I must begin by saying how vital I think it is, whenever any professional body is considering the question of professional negligence and claims, to keep one's eye and one's mind on the real questions; and these are not questions about liability, they are questions about what is the true and proper function of, in your case, the accountant. In other words, for what do you intend to be responsible? This is because I presume that, as professional people, you see yourselves as performing a useful function, as undertaking responsibility. If you do not keep your mind on that primary question it is very easy to become obsessed with negative and rather defensive stratagems designed to limit liability; and in doing that there will be a tendency to cut back on your proper role and to limit the usefulness of the performance of a job that needs doing. Let us take a particular case: the broad one of the duty of care that is owed. Surely, a professional man must approach the question of whose interests he should have in mind or what steps he ought to take. He should approach that from the angle of defining his true function and

---

[*] This chapter is based on a transcript of a talk by W D Prosser, edited by Professor Nobes, and checked by Dean Prosser.

not from the angle of trying to avoid some eventual liability if he gets it wrong. Liability, I would suggest, is merely the dark side of fulfilling a proud and responsible function and being willing to answer for things one has undertaken to do.

I would like to start by considering how things stand in the United Kingdom at present on keeping a proper relationship between the liability that the law demands of professional people and the primary role which they have which that liability ought to reflect. I say the UK because, in my view, the law of Scotland and the law south of the border on questions of professional liability has now come, probably from rather different directions, to be effectively the same. And I think it is therefore on that scale that one is trying to see how much the law, and in particular, recent decisions, have kept these two aspects (of the primary role and liability) properly synchronised.

What is the general basis on which a person may be held liable for his professional acts? Obviously the root of any such liability will be his contract. It is only when he is hired by someone to do something that these questions will normally arise and, historically at least, that has given rise to a good deal of litigation, and attempts by the court to define what the accountant was meant to be doing. I think that that sort of problem is less likely to arise now because the profession has put its mind to improving and standardising its terms of engagement. Is he to be an auditor; is he to fulfil some lesser role; if he is an auditor, what particular things has he undertaken? Most of these doubts are now of the past. As far as contracts are concerned, it is perhaps more in the expanding fields of advisory work that there may still be problems for the profession as to quite what the terms should be. Now of course some tasks are not merely a matter of private contract, but become a matter of accepting what one can call a public office, as a receiver, a liquidator, or the like. In those cases there will not be just a letter of engagement, but statutory responsibilities for breach of which there may be statutory consequences. However, I propose to stick to the accountant practising as such rather than the accountant who has undertaken one of these statutory offices, although much that applies to the one also applies to the other.

Apart from these special tasks that are undertaken, it is also the case that in any ordinary contract there will be implied duties as well as the specific terms describing the job.[1] These implied duties are owed by the accountant to the person or body who employs him, but there are also implied general duties owed to others who are not in contract with him. Most particularly, of course, there is the obligation to exercise reasonable care, and the implied undertaking that one will act according to the reasonable standards of a competent member of one's profession. The obligations of a professional man will vary with two matters: first, according to who his client is and, second, according to his own specialities. It has been said in the legal context that if the lawyer, who ought to be learned, advises a lay client, who he knows is wholly ignorant, then he will be responsible on a wider basis than when he is advising a lay client who is known to be better informed.

There is of course the possibility of including in a contract terms which cut down one's obligations or cut down one's liability.[2] Whether one is talking of express obligations or implied obligations it is possible, subject to certain statutory limits, to contract out of undertaking particular things and possibly in some circumstances to contract out of liability for mistakes. However, quite apart from the statutory restraints, I would suggest that that in principle should be something that one tries not to embark upon. If one has correctly defined the role that one intends to play and if one has left out obligations that one does not intend to undertake, then one should not have to face up to refusing to accept responsibility for what has been undertaken. This limitation of liability is probably an avenue one should try not to go down, but to stick to defining the true and proper task and accepting responsibility for that according to the rules that govern it. Of course, it would be proper to leave out particular obligations but one would be doing that because they are inappropriate not because it is unsafe to take them on.[3]

The other way of limiting liability in a contract will be some kind of express statement that it is only for particular uses or for the eyes of particular people, with a view to at least excluding claims by people beyond that defined circle. However, again, I would suggest that this is probably not something which you can rely on much in the ordinary practice of the profession. This is because many of the functions of an accountant are necessarily and by definition public matters and many others relate to situations where, even without a statutory need for a document being public, the whole purpose of giving the advice is precisely so that it can be shown to people other than the client, and used for wider purposes. So, I would suggest, again, that so far as the contract is concerned and so far as liability to outsiders is concerned, it is important simply to decide what it is that one is doing and not to erect defences for protective purposes.

I have already mentioned this question of the circle of people who will want to see the product and I now turn to the specific question of the scope of obligation. To whom does a professional man, particularly the accountant, owe duties? To whom will he be liable if he breaches such duties? As a general statement, where one has a contract as the basis for a particular job, it has for a very long time been plain that the product of one's work is something that one can be liable for, not merely to the client or the employer, but to other people under a general duty of care. In broad terms that obligation has been described as an obligation owed to one's neighbour, and one's neighbour has been defined as a person who will foreseeably be affected by one's actions.[4]

Initially at least, in this country, an

attempt was made to be more protective to the
professional man, the adviser, and not to burden
him with this general duty to any category or
class of persons who might foreseeably be
affected, but only to make him liable to the
person with whom he had a contract and to another
limited category of people with whom there was
what was called a special relationship.[5]   An
auditor of accounts would be liable, for example,
not merely to the company, but perhaps to its
existing shareholders as people that plainly would
be interested, perhaps to other actual people
involved, perhaps an actual lender or perhaps to
someone who was known to be contemplating a
takeover.   However, for want of a special
relationship, the auditor would probably have
been free of duties to a wider class.   Now, what
has changed, and I think inevitably changed
because it was not workable, is that the duty
owed by a professional man has come to be the same
as, or very close to, the general rule that one is
liable to all those who reasonable foresight would
tell you might be affected by your actions.
Certainly, in the most recent cases both in
England (the Jeb Fasteners case)[6] and in Scotland
(the case called Twomax),[7] it is now plain that
the liability in terms of the people to whom a
duty is owed is very wide indeed.   It really has
come to be that virtually anyone may see and make
use of any document which gets out of the safe and
becomes available in a more public way.   And it
will often be quite impracticable to take
protective measures against that, if one is to
preserve the function that is being performed.
It has been suggested by the judges that there
will perhaps be limiting factors but I fear that
one has to take that with something of a pinch of
salt and that it really will be all those who
might be affected.
    The remaining protections will be questions
of evidence: whether a particular individual did
in fact rely on a given statement or document,
whether there is in fact a causal connection
between his loss and the mistake or omission
that the accountant has made.   It seems to me

45

that, for the future, one must accept that it will
very seldom be a defence to say "I owed him no
duty". If someone can show a causal connection
then it is likely that you will have to accept
that you did owe a duty to almost anyone.

I would like to turn now to the standard of
performance, in particular in relation to the
obligations of care. What sort of standard does
one have to fulfil? I have already mentioned
that the standard in general is that of a
reasonably competent practitioner. There has
been no real shift in recent times in that
although, particularly in one or two the medical
cases, there have been indications on the part of
the court that even where a doctor can show that
what he did was standard practice, nonetheless
the court might say that it is not a proper
practice,[8] that is not what the profession owes to
its customers, victims, whatever. Therefore, it
could be that there is no defence even where
standard practice can be pointed to. However, in
general I think it remains true that if you can
invoke the practice of your peers then you should
not be held to be negligent.[9] Indeed, apart from
the example that I have just given of a sort of
generally improper practice, it can be said that,
perhaps as a result of looking across the Atlantic
at what is perceived to be happening there, the
courts here have strengthened their protection
of a professional's right to make a proper
professional judgement, the freedom to judge
according to one's own lights. Particularly in
medical cases, it has been stressed that not all
errors are negligence.[10] In another case it has
been shown that if you get a clash of two
respectable opinions from the profession, the
court should not simply choose one and say it is
right and anything else is negligent.[11] It
should accept merely that there is doubt and that
both the conflicting courses may be tenable
without negligence.

Looking beyond medicine, there has been a
case in which broker advice on commodities was
held to be a matter of judgement; admittedly it
was a fairly extreme proposition that the broker

should be liable virtually if the client lost at
all in any circumstances. But, nonetheless, the
principle is confirmed that, on matters of advice
and judgement, it is very unlikely that negligence
will arise across a wide range; and more
generally it has been stressed that in relation to
professional work (with medicine, architecture and
the law being mentioned) proof of negligence will
be very hard. I think it is implicit in that
general statement that the same would apply to
accountants. Specifically, however, I think that
one has to be more depressing in relation to
accountants because it is not so clear from the
cases which have involved accountants that
judgement can be exercised as freely as in these
other professions without liability for mistakes.
The old situation where the auditor was a watchdog
and not a bloodhound has in my view shifted fairly
significantly. One starts as a watchdog, but
with very wide open ears and eyes and with the
need to transform oneself into a fairly suspicious
bloodhound fairly quickly. There is now seen to
be an obligation on an accountant to be suspicious
not merely that a mistake may have been made but
that there has been dishonesty. I think it may
become a problem to try to hold a line as to just
how much one is expected to suspect dishonesty as
well as error.

Against that background, with the wide range
of people to whom one owes a duty now, with the
greater availability of information, the risks
do seem to be rising. The question arises
whether the increased demands which are made by
the law are right in terms of the role which an
accountant intends to fulfil or whether they are
unfair and producing a discrepancy between the
demands of the law and the intentional
responsibilities of the accountant. I suggest
that these increased demands of the law are in
general fair, and that what they are doing is
reflecting an increasing willingness by
accountants to dig deeper and to advise more
widely, as the world becomes more complex and
information more readily available in volume. At
least to my eye there is not a serious

discrepancy between the legal responsibility that is demanded and the professional responsibility that is asserted. It means, of course, that reliance on others becomes harder and harder; for example, reliance on the verbal explanations of a director is less likely to be acceptable; it would be expected that some kind of documentary vouching would be carried out. However, it may be the ability of the accountant to take on a heavier load and his willingness to fulfil a rather wider function that has brought about in part the increased demands of the law. Also, of course, with changes in statutory requirements and the powers of digging that go with that, the law is likely to be saying increasingly: "if you can, you must". If you can discover X, it is likely that you should discover X. Thus, while I think there is an increased load of responsibility, this is so in both senses: the responsibilities intentionally undertaken as well as the responsibilities which one bears when things go wrong.

I would like to turn to a specific aspect of recent years which has altered and is likely to alter further the sort of responsibilities that are imposed on accountants by the law, and that is the whole question of the rules, codes and practices laid down by the profession for its members. Again, this is not of course special to accountants, it is a matter that affects all professions in one way or another. The existence of specific rules plainly opens up a possibility of much more precise claims for negligence because there can be a claim for negligence based on the failure to comply with what has become a specific rule. It will not just be a case of failure to comply with generally recognised precautions which can be a matter of argument, but failure to comply with something in black and white. One conclusion from that is that one should not have rules. In a sense that has been the attitude of my own profession so far; we justify it by saying that we really know all these rules by the light of reason, tradition and so forth. However, we are considering having stated rules, and I suggest that in the bigger professions this is appropriate, not as something to do with liability, but for the positive purposes of the profession. It is in the interests of the profession to try to raise its standards by stating them; it is in the interests of the clients that the standards should be known and that proper practice should be available and familiar. If that is so, in the primary interest of the profession one should not tear them up in order to remove the handholds of those who want to put forward claims.

Nonetheless, the proliferation of rules and practices gives rise to a real risk that the tail may wag the dog, the risk that the highly competent and imaginative leader of new thinking in the profession may be unfairly and undesirably required to conform. Such a leader may be told that he has failed to comply with rules when really it is the rules that are failing to comply with him. Rules may imply rigidity and a static situation as regards proper practice which should not be the case in any profession. And that is my concern about these rules: that if they are stated too dogmatically and stated as applicable to everyone, then they will leave people exposed to criticism and at risk in the courts when they should not be. Professionals will have lost their freedom of judgement, and thus have thrown away the fundamentals of being a professional. However, one may be able to avoid this by not making rules as rules but by talking in terms of guidelines, recommendations or statements of normal practice and thus hope at least to deprive the claimant of the power to say that everyone who breaks it must be wrong.

There is some comfort in recent authority in relation to architects (a Scots case)[12] where the architects in question had ignored a British Standard Code of Practice provision and came to court willing to say: "Indeed, we do not do that; that kind of statement is merely a statement of what in general the writers of it, a committee, think is done. We do not do it; other leading architects do not do it. We think it is wrong, and we are sure that in time the committees will reflect our practice in the rules". At the initial fatal accident enquiry and subsequent proof the court would not accept this. However, at appeal the court did; and I regard that as of some significance in preserving one from the unfortunate results of rules.

I have been talking about what the duties, and the scope of one's duties, will be seen as being by the courts. I have suggested that you probably cannot hope that these can be restrained; that there just is a wider exposure. Now I turn to the consequences of that in court or if a claim is asserted. There is a need not to deny that one owed a duty, not to say that the standards are deficient, but simply to get back to the need of evidence of the facts of the particular case. If a negligence claim is made there are certain crucial matters which the object of the claim, the accountant, will have to consider; and here I am rather more uneasy at some indications that the courts are too willing to use hindsight in judging causation and in judging whether there was a failure. It is true that in the Jeb Fasteners case[13] the court was willing to see a causal break, in other words that there was error but that it did not lead to the results. However, in the Twomax case[14] which I mentioned earlier it did seem that the court was willing to draw inferences that there had been a failure in the accounts of an earlier year from material relating to later years; it was willing apparently to infer that there must have been a different position from that which was shown in the accounts. That seems to run dangerously close to an idea that there is a guarantee of performance that, if things go wrong subsequently, then there must have been some error further back; dangerously close to expecting too much and seeing a causal connection where that is not appropriate.

On the matter of reliance on relatively old information, it may be difficult to say that a claimant was beyond the category of people to whom one would owe a duty, if he was looking at the accounts, but it will be very important to try to prove as a matter of fact that he simply was not relying on the information. These are the sort of problems, purely factual problems, which will face an accountant and where I am somewhat pessimistic as to whether the courts are appreciative enough of the dangers of using hindsight. Coupled with this is the question of how much the accountant will be expected to warn as to the future. Up to a point, you can cover that in terms of engagement. Nonetheless, it will be a problem because he who assesses a present situation inevitably has a view as to a future situation by inference. In medical cases the need to inform the patient has become a pretty contentious field of law, that turns on surgical and other treatment which would otherwise be an assault. This is a matter of consent, which is a quite different legal matter from the accountant's position. However, this may spill over, such that it will be expected of accountants that they should have said more than has been customary.

The other field that I should mention is the case of giving advice and, particularly, tax planning or corporate planning advice. There is an increasing difficulty related to moving beyond one's own speciality or even beyond one's own profession. I am not suggesting that every accountant has to consult a lawyer every time that there is a legal aspect to his advice. Nonetheless, he will be entitled to do that and the danger is that the courts will take the line that I have suggested already: "if you can, you must". That is, there may be difficulty if you get something wrong on law and could have taken a lawyer's advice. I wonder whether in these fields one may need, like architects, to create some kind of design team which may involve more than one profession in order to ensure that there is an allocation of responsibility within a particular branch of a profession or even beyond that profession. This is not an attractive prospect, since much accountancy advice on law is plainly highly skilled. Nonetheless, where it is a matter of legal interpretation, the case law is not very comforting for the accountant who goes beyond his professional qualification.

In general, the widening exposure to claims of negligence is broadly correlative to a very proper broadening of function and performance and, despite some of the problems about establishing what the proper facts are and getting proper judgements as to whether there is fault, the increased exposure is not really to be deplored. It really ought to be accepted as the other side of one's increasing responsibilities; accepted and, if possible, insured against.

Notes

(1) See also Oliver J, <u>Midland Bank v Hett, Stubbs & Kemp</u> (1979) Ch 434.

(2) See Hedley Byrne - the avoidance of liability because of a disclaimer.

(3) See also <u>Professional Liability of Accountants and Auditors</u>, Guidance for members in practice, issued by the Institute of Chartered Accountants in England and Wales, November 1983.

(4) See Lord Atkin's neighbourhood test in <u>Donoghue v Stevenson</u> (1932) AC, p 580.

(5) Hedley Byrne & Co Ltd v Heller & Partners Ltd (1964) AC 465.

(6) <u>Jeb Fasteners Ltd v Marks Bloom & Co</u> (1981) 3 all ER 289.

(7) <u>Twomax Ltd & Ors v Dickson MacFarlane & Robinson</u>, Opinion of Lord Stewart in the Court of Session (Outer House) Edinburgh (1982).

(8) See <u>Clarke v Adams</u> (1950) 94 SJ 599.

(9) McNair J in <u>Bolam v Friern Hospital Management Committee</u> (1957) 1 WLR 582 : "... is not guilty of negligence if he has acted in accordance with a practice accepted as proper by a responsible body of medical men skilled in that particular art".

(10) Denning L J, <u>Hatcher v Black</u>, The Times, July 2 1954 : "You must not, therefore, find him negligent simply because something happens to go wrong".

(11) Lord Clyde in <u>Hunter v Hanley</u> (1955) SC 200: "In the realm of diagnosis and treatment there is ample scope for genuine difference of opinion and one man clearly is not negligent merely because his conclusion differs from that of other professional men, nor because he has displayed less skill or knowledge than others have done".

(12) <u>Kelly v City of Edinburgh District Council</u> (1982) S LT, 593.

(13) As note 5.

(14) As note 6.

Chapter Five

PROFESSIONAL INDEMNITY

Peter Christie[*]

I will start by trying to give you a backdrop to the insurance market so that you may have a better understanding of the specifics of professional indemnity insurance. It is recognised that the insurance market generally, in all classes of business, is driven by supply and demand. It is, therefore, very cyclical in its pricing and availability. We are currently in the doldrums world-wide, and in one of the most competitive insurance markets ever seen and that is having a depressing effect on the pricing of insurance and is increasing its availability. However, this may be dangerous in terms of lulling one into a false sense of security as to its continued availability. The historic perception of those in the market place is that these conditions will not only cease to exist but will reverse. Nevertheless, there is debate as to whether we might have had a change in the structure of the insurance market world-wide; whether perhaps that cycle will not continue as it has over the last fifty years. This arises from another factor that bears directly on professional indemnity, which is the intense internationalisation of the insurance market.

* This chapter is based on a transcript of a talk by Peter Christie, edited by Professor Nobes, and checked by Mr Christie.

Probably in the last ten years, the participation of foreign insurers in all the major markets of the world has increased dramatically. European insurers are writing large amounts of foreign business; they have entered the United States in a major way, and US insurers have entered Europe in a major way. However, the international market is still substantially US driven. Something like 45 per cent of the world's property-casualty insurance premiums are still generated in the United States. Given this and the highly international market place, events in the US are going to have a direct impact on availability and price throughout the world.

Let us now examine those features of professional indemnity insurance that are unique. First, it is a very obscure and difficult type of coverage for most insurance underwriters. It may be easy to understand how likely it is that a house is going to fall down or burn; it is even fairly easy to understand why more people were killed on the roads this year than last year. However, it is very arcane why more lawyers were sued this year than last year. Most insurance underwriters have a fear of their inability to understand what is driving the market, what is driving the losses. The second part of that is the inability to evaluate what the cost of any given event or claim may be. This exists in most types of liability insurance, but it is particularly acute in the professional liability area. The major problem is that there is a dual level of argument: first, did the events take place and, secondly, what is the value of the damage? This is different from an automobile accident, where it can usually be agreed whether a man is dead.

This leads to another problem: that the insurance market perceives professional indemnity to be what we call "long-tail". That is, when you price a product or sell a policy in 1985, which will insure the claims asserted against you in 1985, you have to recognise that it is possible that you will not pay out those claims for 5 or 10 years. We have open claims in one of our areas of concentration, the international accounting firms, that are 15 years old. It is fairly terrifying for an insurer to have to price his widget today when he will not know for 15 years what that widget will cost him; and this is part of his inability to evaluate it. Of course, there is an offset against that, which has been insufficiently recognised by the insurance market but will be recognised more in the future, and this is the high investment income from the premiums that the insurer is holding for the period before he has to pay out. The insurance business has considered over the last ten years that it has a special status in the world, such that this investment income is just something that can be put in the back pocket and that there is an entitlement to make an underwriting profit as well. However, that is changing; the high interest rates of the last few years, the increased sophistication of insurance buyers and the use of mutual insurance companies have changed dramatically. So I think that the benefit of this will be seen more in the premium structure for professional firms, and it is a very very material benefit.

These concerns have had an impact on the market for professional indemnity that has made it, in world terms, a very small market. The number of insurers who are willing to write professional indemnity is small. It also has a feature that is extremely worrying and could be a cause of a collapse of availability and pricing for professional indemnity insurance: the temptation for insurers to indulge in predatory pricing. Take the insurer who has been told to increase his premium income, and suppose that he is insuring houses. If he undercharges, when the underwriting losses come in, it is very difficult for him to say that he charged low premiums because he had a message from heaven that there were going to be fewer houses burning down next year in England. However, it is easier in indemnity to say that you have analysed all the soft trends, looked at the quality of the firms, the quality of the profession, and at how the

losses are going, and then to convince yourself
that you are on to a great game. One of the
adages of the professional liability business is
that you should never employ an underwriter over
the age of 50 because he will be dead by the time
the losses come in. There is much truth in that;
you can get away with it for a long time. Thus,
predatory pricing is probably one of the reasons
for the problems of the last few years in
professional indemnity. When top management of a
company see this area as being their big loss (a
problem which arises 5 years after they have
written the business) they get out of it and do
not touch that business again for another five
years. This has a long-term effect on the market.

The next thing that might be useful to those
involved in buying insurance for your firms is to
touch upon two or three items in the policy
wording that need particular attention. The
first point is to ask what exactly does a policy
for a period, say, the calendar year 1985, cover?
In most countries and in most professions the
policy will cover two events. It will cover any
matter where you believe a claim might arise,
provided that you notify it to the insurer during
that period. It will also cover any claim made
against you during that period where you had no
previous perception that there might be a problem.
Now this gives rise to a major problem. It means
that the insurance you buy this year is probably
not going to cover what you do this year. It
covers mistakes that you become aware of or claims
made against you this year. In the event that
you cannot renew the policy at the end of the
period, you have no guarantee in most cases in
professional liability that you are covered for
evermore for acts committed whilst you have the
policy. This is particularly a problem for sole
practitioners who may retire.

The reason for this structure is that without
it we probably would not have an insurance market
at all. The other way that it used to be done,
particularly in the United States, was to write
policies that did cover the acts committed during
the currency of the policy. However, given that

there may be a 5 to 10 year delay between the notification of a claim and the disposition of that matter, if the policy gives cover on the basis of when the act was committed, there is an exceptionally long period before the losses are determined. In the early 1970s, the insurance market found a total inability to handle that. The second item relates to the notification of circumstances or losses. I would urge anyone who has responsibility in this area to be very clear what it is you are required to notify to the insurers. In many cases there will be a requirement that you notify an insurer of any circumstance that may give rise to a claim. Probably the safest thing to do is to empty your entire filing system on to the underwriter's desk at every renewal date. More practically, you would certainly be wise to leave a paper trail of good faith effort, and to have internal systems that alert staff to the necessity of advising the appropriate partner of matters that may give rise to a claim. The other matter that you should look at is <u>who</u> you have to notify, particularly if you are buying what is known in the UK as "top-up insurance". You may encounter circumstances where there is a different notification requirement on the excess coverage.

The next point is the question of fraud coverage. The best that you will probably get from an insurance policy is that, first, it will insure you for successful actions for fraud in the event that it was not held that you had actual <u>intent</u> to deceive or defraud. That gives you some protection. The second thing, and you should look for this very carefully, is that you can also get policies that will protect the innocent partners in the event of another partner's fraud; and that is obviously essential coverage which many policies do not have.

There are some related issues that are quite interesting. The question is becoming more and more frequently posed, and I have particular familiarity with this in Canada, of whether it is possible to insure intentional acts. In Canada, both under common law and under statutory law, it is contrary to public policy to give insurance for the expected result of a wrongful act. This is not quite as bad as it sounds because you have not only to commit the wrongful act but you also have to have expected it to cause harm to someone. To date in Canada the courts have held that this is not an insurable issue. This is frightening when it gets to the point of considering the liability of the innocent partners. To date, there has not been a conclusive case on this.

This relates to the matter of punitive damages in the United States, where the same sort of public policy issues have been raised. Is it proper that you can buy insurance which in effect avoids the intent of the law, ie to punish you in punitive damages? You cannot insure against a speeding fine. Turning to consumer laws, there was a case[1] in Massachusetts (which has a consumer protection law which was not originally thought to apply to lawyers) in which a lawyer, after an act of negligence, was sued under the Consumer Protection Law; that gave the plaintiff treble damages. This was probably originally intended to apply to door-to-door salesmen, but is being applied to law firms. Similarly, the federal statute[2] on anti-racketeering has treble damages in it, and is being applied to accountants. This question of statutarily increased damages is a difficult one for the insurance industry. You should at least make sure that your insurance policy does cover an innocent partner for another partner's fraud.

The next area is the question of geographical restrictions. Some people are a little blase when they see a restriction on their policy concerning suits in the USA or Australia. However, you may find that you have much more potential exposure to overseas suits than you might have thought; you do not need to be in the USA to have the exposure, you do not even need a US client. If you have lenders who are from the USA, or if your client is raising money in the USA, there is a potential for US jurisdiction. The other part of this, which has been a hot issue for some medium-sized accounting firms, concerns international associations with colleagues in another country. Do you incur a liability for their acts? I think most lawyers will certainly not tell you that you cannot be liable for their acts, and this is a potential problem where there is any sort of international relationship.

The final point on policy wording concerns the breadth of services. Many insurance policies will say that they cover the insured in his professional capacity as an accountant. We became aware of a case where an accountant was sued on the basis of his management services advice and the insurer turned down the claim because it did not concern his capacity as an accountant. The client ultimately won the case, but I think there are clear problems as the accounting profession begins to move into other areas; executive recruiting, for example. Many insurers do not recognise the breadth of services that a modern accounting firm is providing.

Let us consider proposal forms. Insurance contracts made in good faith entail an obligation to reveal anything material, even if you are not asked the question. There may be a particular problem where you are asked: "are you aware of any circumstances that may give rise to a claim?". Deal with that very carefully indeed. With 20/20 hindsight, when the problem comes up a year later, the insurer is going to look at the proposal form and ask: "did he know about this when he signed this proposal form?". The other area that you should be concerned about, particularly if you are in a multi-partner firm, is the truth of the statements on the proposal form. This is serious, if there is a partner who was indulging in some type of fraud, yet was the partner who completed the proposal form. The insurers will take the position, with some backing in law, that if the applicant signed the proposal form knowing that it was incorrect to deny knowledge of any circumstances that might give rise to a claim, they can void the entire policy as to all insureds. This can be horrifying in the fidelity area, where the very thing you are buying insurance for is the event that voids the insurance.

Let us turn to one of the big issues in the United States which has almost been resolved now. That is the question of whether a lawyer is in a position of conflict when he is representing, in a professional liability claim or any other claim, both the insured and the insurer. The problem is that the lawyer is meant to be advising the insured as to how best to perfect his claim and to be advising the insurer as to what his rights are. I have great difficulty in seeing how any professional advisor can deal with those two things together. It is a problem that I think has been resolved in North America in that it does not now happen. However, it is common in Australia and the UK, and you should be very alert to it if you have the unfortunate experience of becoming involved in a claim.

A further matter, that has become a very acute problem in the United States, concerns bad faith issues between the insured and the insurer. The insurer owes to the insured an obligation to deal with him in good faith. To take a simple example, suppose that the insured has $1 million coverage, but is being sued for $20 million. He can settle it for $1 million, but the insurer makes him fight the claim. Suppose, however, that there is a $20 million judgement, followed by the insurer offering to pay the one million and leave the 19 million for the insured to pay. The courts in the USA have considered that offensive, and have found against the insurers.

The other issue, and this comes back to the policy wording, concerns the case where the insurer wants to settle and you do not. You should look at your policy closely and make sure what your rights are in that circumstance. Insurers are split on their general attitude to the question of whether to pay up and get out quick, or whether to fight every case. Those insurers who are not particularly committed to, or expert in, the professional indemnity market have a tendency to pay quick and get out. That makes economic sense from their point of view; cases rarely get better, they usually get worse. The more sophisticated recognise some very severe dangers, which were clear in the United States in the late 1960s and early 1970s. That is, if you generate a public perception that an accounting firm is a soft touch, it is going to cost a lot more in the long run than losing badly on one or two cases. In the US they perhaps have a greater problem with this; the extensive use of juries makes it very difficult to predict outcomes. This can still be a problem even in the UK, Canada and Australia, where litigation is before a judge but is still uncertain. So it is a difficult decision whether to fight or not, and it can be very expensive to get it wrong. I hope that the large settlements in the UK, Australia and the United States as a result of adverse court decisions will not cause the profession and insurers to get scared of taking cases through to final disposition.

Turning to another point, generally an ambiguous insurance contract is construed against the insurer as being the author and seller of the contract. There have been attacks on that theory in the United States on the grounds that, where the buyer has competent legal counsel, competent insurance brokers, and perhaps an insurance manager, that changes the process because there is equal bargaining. So, if you are negotiating with your insurance broker, how much should you get involved in drafting the policy wording? The contract should not be allowed to become _your_ contract.

The next area to consider is compulsory insurance. Looking first at the legal profession, as a comparison to the accounting profession, in the UK there is a compulsory insurance programme, insured in the commercial market with one insurer. That I believe was generated originally by perception of the need to assure the public of the existence of insurance. Ontario, which has the largest number of lawyers in Canada, has a compulsory insurance programme, a self-insured mutual fund. The United States has no compulsory insurance requirements for attorneys. There is fierce competition at the

63

moment amongst insurers and the rates are low. Australian states have compulsory commercial insurance for lawyers.

However, the accountancy profession is different. Although there is a high proportion of compulsory insurance in the legal professions around the world, there are only two exceptions to its absence for accountants. One exception is that for membership of the SEC practice section of the American Institute there are some minimum requirements for insurance but no means to check that they are being followed nor any attempt by the Institute to provide the insurance themselves. The other exceptions are Germany and France, where everyone buys insurance from a pool negotiated by the Institutes.

The next area is the size of coverage to buy. A starting point could be to ask how big a claim one could have, perhaps to look at one's largest fee and then triple it. However, I do not see a relationship between the amount of the fee and the potential liability. There might on occasion be a relationship between what the fee should have been, had you done all the work you should do, and the potential liability! In the USA, people have looked to the market value of the shares of a client. However, first of all this is very frightening; and, secondly, it is not often practical to try to buy insurance on those levels. I have an example on this subject of a client, a fairly small accounting firm, who was the auditor of a construction company which had small net assets but completion bonds on construction of $50 million from an insurance company. It collapsed and the insurer paid the $50 million, and sued the accounting firm on the basis that the insurer had issued the bonds after examining the financial statements.[3] The point is that the loss bore no relationship to the size of the company they were auditing or to its revenue.

What you can look at is the largest claim ten years ago, five years ago and today, and you will find some terrifying answers anywhere in the world. The problem is that you make a decision this year on the claim that is ultimately going to come to court in three years time and may be settled or come to judgement another year after that. You have to think forward. I suppose the answer is that you had better buy as much as you can afford.

The last area I wanted to touch on is a matter that has been interesting us in Canada, but which is applicable to the UK. This concerns the liability arising out of insolvencies, where the accountant is acting as the receiver manager or trustee. Historically in Canada much lending was done by the banks, who also appointed receivers. The bank used to be prepared to totally indemnify the accountant. However, that has broken down to a substantial degree, such that the accountant may now be subject to litigation.

The other area that worries us as insurance brokers concerns a case such as the following. Suppose that an accountant is acting as a receiver; he has single signature authority over an account with £20 million in it; he pulls out the money and runs off to South America. Is this a professional indemnity claim or a fidelity claim? Its professional indemnity character will be questioned in such a circumstance, where it is clearly a cash theft. The insurers may argue that they intended only to cover professional failure.

The other point that worries us is cover for activities arising out of the business management of an insolvent company. It might be claimed that a liquidator was mispricing the assets being sold. I think that is covered under most professional indemnity policies, but there may be difficulties here in future if there are large claims.

Next, how is the insurance product priced? It is very difficult for insurers to price this type of product. There is no hard base from which to project losses; there is a long tail and various other features that make it very hard to establish any sound actuarial base. This will be affected by environmental changes; for example, by the public's perception of the responsibility of auditors, by the state of the economy (a recessive economy leads to increased losses), by changes in law and by a growing consumer orientation. However, there are some touchstones that almost all insurers use in trying to develop pricing. The choice usually is to price the coverage for a professional firm either based on fees or based on personnel. Nevertheless, there may not be much difference at the end of the day, because the underwriter is looking for a certain amount of money and he will come up with the rate that will achieve it.

The other matter that insurers look at is specialisation. They have done this more for solicitors than for accountants. Some area will be noted as being particularly hazardous; for example, patent law. This can have an impact by spreading premiums differently amongst different firms, but the statistical base is so thin that it is hard to say that tax is half as liable as audit, etc. The insurance business would love to run your profession to the extent of picking pieces of a composite firm and charging more for certain parts. However, it is then a short step to a refusal to insure certain activities. I think the professions are well served by accepting a fairly rough-and-ready approach from the insurers as a trade off for keeping them out of trying to tell you how to run your business.

More important than all this is an understanding of what is really driving the pricing in professional liability. At the end of the day, insurance is a pool. One cannot sensibly say that one does not want to pay for the other man's losses. The person who has the losses wins, the person who does not have the losses loses. The key point in terms of premium generation by the insurers for professional firms is to identify what pool is being used. We do not know the answer to that as brokers, and essentially it is not within our control. Thus, there are large elements of your insurance premium that are not due to your own losses, and it is unrealistic to ask why one's premium rises even though one has not had a loss. Insurance should not, in my view, be a product that you cannot afford to buy the moment it has worked. Many insurers would like to see it in that position. I think that is an important point for any of you who are involved in negotiating for the Institute or for your firms.

There is another problem with what we call "loss-loading", charging people more money if they have had losses. What do you do about the insured who spends his £20,000 on successfully defending a suit? Is he a bad guy or a good guy? You do not know whether he would have won or not. It is very difficult to get any realistic rating out of that. It raises an issue that is very important. We often have people saying to us that the insurers should not protect bad work; that some professionals are doing a sloppy job on a cheaper fee just because they have insurance. The suggestion is that such professionals should be put out of business, by raising the price of insurance to such a level that they cannot buy any. However, do you really want the insurers to be the disciplinarians of your profession? That would become extremely uncomfortable because their competence to do that is minimal. They are going to attack the wrong people.

Let us now make predictions about supply and demand. You must recognise that the US experience will affect UK insurance rates. The insurers will ask why a huge loss in New York today will not be repeated as a loss in London tomorrow. The market place is international, it knows about losses in New York or Australia or Singapore. It does recognise big differentials of degree of exposure, but it will be made nervous by what is happening elsewhere. There is reason to believe that the situation in the United Kingdom as far as accountants' liability is concerned is deteriorating. Two elements of the problem in the UK are that it is a relatively small premium base, compared to the USA and that it is also in a transition period in terms of its liabilities. Underwriters can underwrite anything as long as it is predictable. In the United States it has become to a degree predictable; perhaps

predictably bad, but predictable. Underwriters
can make money on predictable events because they
know what to charge. In the United Kingdom
underwriters may be beginning to believe that they
are in such a rapidly changing situation that they
have no ability to predict and therefore no
ability to price. That is what happened in the
late 1960s in the United States when many
accounting firms could not buy insurance at any
price.

So, will there be a crisis of availability
and cost of professional indemnity insurance, as
has happened in the United States? What are the
insurers concerns? Obviously, their primary
concern is that professional liabilities may be
expanding due to the degree of competition in the
profession, and that this may be beginning to
lower standards. They are also very concerned
about the changing financial markets,
computerisation and different financing methods.
It is a complex world, and there is concern about
how well auditors and accountants understand that
world. The world banking system is obviously
frightening for the insurers of professionals.
Legal costs continue to worry them. Their
concern is not with the level of legal fees but
with the uncontrolled type of litigation in
professional liability cases. There is a case in
Australia with Cambridge Credit where the trial
must have been on and off now for two years.

The final underwriter concern is "the deep
pocket theory", which is shorthand to describe a
case where the company is bankrupt, the directors
are in Costa 'Rica, and the only party involved
with any money is the accounting firm. I would
now overlay that concern with a trend that has
begun in the USA and may be illustrated by a New
Jersey case[4] where Touche Ross were the
defendants. The judge held that it was suitable
for the accountants to be liable because they
could buy insurance and had got insurance, and
that insurance is a good mechanism to spread the
risk of investment throughout society. This is
a terrifying suggestion, but there is strong
pressure to make the securities market safe for

the public. However, the result could be that the insurers deem the profession to be uninsurable. Nevertheless, I think the profession is large enough to bear the cost ultimately of the liabilities they will probably face; and the insurance market is also large enough. Ultimately, you can pass the costs on to the people who should be paying for them, and are getting the benefit: the clients.

With a high commitment to quality control, with sensitivity to client selection at the front end, with support by the profession for a rational fee structure and insurance price structure, and with increasing officers' liability insurance for corporations (so that there are some other deep pockets around), I believe there will be a continuing affordable insurance market.

Notes

(1) 535 F. Supp 1125.
(2) Corrupt Organizations Act, 18 USC, SS 1961-1968 (1982).
(3) <u>JF White Engineering Corporation et al v General Insurance Co of America</u>, 351 F 2d 231.
(4) In Re : Data Access Systems Security litigation. Unreported (Lexis - Masterfile 81-1923).

Chapter Six

A VIEW FROM THE USA

Richard Murray[*]

I expect that by the end of the day those of you who had the courage to come will recognise that, although you Scots created the profession, somewhere along the line the rest of us have mucked it up and are bringing it back to your shores not looking quite as you exported it.

It was almost to the day ten years ago that the North American legal and accounting professions first recognised the opening of the professional liability risk floodgates by holding a conference in Montreal that was designed as a first attempt to reconcile views and figure out what to do about it. Some of us must have taught very well because the past ten years have not been quiet times for us in North America.

You will be aware that we went through a serious crisis in the profession in the late 1960s, though not properly recognised until the early part of the 1970s; a crisis of insurability, a crisis of manageability, of focus, and in some instances a crisis of the survivability of individual firms or the shape of the profession. We weathered that with a little luck and a little skill, and we entered a stable period where the claims phenomenon was a serious part of our

---

[*] This chapter is based on a transcript of a talk by Rick Murray, edited by Professor Nobes, and checked by Mr Murray.

business, but not one that engaged daily headlines.

However, North America is recognising now a new wave of difficulty, largely precipitated by the aftermath of the depression we have been through, which has produced a level of significant cases that we have not known for the last 6 or 7 years. That is frightening to those of us who understand how burdensome a case can be. You may remember the consequence of the Fund of Funds litigation and the judgement against a firm of nearly $100 million, subsequently settled for an undisclosed amount. That showed what can happen when one elects to roll the dice with a jury trial in a complex commercial and professional setting. We had more evidence this week of how disturbing the environment can be, in a New York litigation involving another accounting firm related to the Saxon Industries debacle. The judge granted a rather unusual request to constitute a class of defendants consisting of all 300 partners of the accounting firm nationwide, on the grounds that it seemed probable that the plaintiffs would receive a judgement so far in excess of the capital and insurance cover of the firm, that it was necessary for protection of the plaintiffs' interests to bring the partners and their personal assets before the court for execution. You may be able to imagine what kind of practice-management consequences that has.

I asked myself why UK professionals might be interested in what is happening in the USA; whether or not there was perhaps some financial stake that crossed the Atlantic. However, I remembered that that could not be the case because when the consequence of the Fund of Funds judgement was current, Ian Hay Davison was asked if he and Arthur Andersen partners in the UK were going to have to pay any part of that judgement; Mr Davison made some comments about the nature of partnership and the fact that it does not extend across the water. Thus, I suspect that your primary interest is in trying to determine why things have become so difficult for our profession in North America, so that you can resist the conditions that would make the burdens as difficult for you. That is an entirely appropriate objective. I will try to define the principal reasons for the problems in the USA and invite you to consider to what degree those conditions either already exist in the United Kingdom or seem to be looming on your shores.

There is a popular assumption in the UK that the problem in the US results from the combined effect of class action privileges and contingent fee opportunities. That theory suggests that it might be simple to stop the problems here. However, the problems in the US are not shareholder problems, certainly not in the litigation environment of the 1980s. The dominant source of litigation in the US is not shareholders, it is not class actions and it is not lawyers operating on contingent fees; it is large institutional investors. The leading insurance companies have tens of billions of dollars in various forms of corporate equities. They do not take kindly to disappointments in their investments, and are most willing to sue the auditors of the companies in which they have invested.

The problems also come from bank financings. Banks in North America are not relaxed today when they find that somebody has taken money out of their pockets; they look to replenish it as fast as possible. We have problems with trustees, liquidators and receivers in their official capacities. We have enormous difficulties with acquisitive companies who were disappointed by the values and results that they acquired. All of those sources of trouble are represented by mainstream counsel who are being paid full rates. They present a far more formidable shape of the enemy today than was the shareholder phenomenon ten years ago; and the responses that are expected from us for professional maintenance in that environment have to be very different. It is a much more challenging environment.

The reasons why a particular piece of litigation comes into existence and why it becomes a threatening problem might be summarised into seven categories. The first, and perhaps dominant one, is consumerism. This is a political theology that is invading every aspect of our life. It is clear that, whether by statute, judicial attitude or social attitude, in any transaction the buyer is the party entitled to protection. The Massachusetts treble damage statute is a burden on the profession as are some other companion state statutes. We have been sued under the Massachusetts treble damage statute by the First National Bank of Boston, just the sort of person you would expect to be protected by a consumer law! For the purchaser, in today's purchasing-oriented environment, risk is becoming one of those unspeakable four-letter words. The guiding principle that governs the normal social and commercial transactions is no longer <u>caveat emptor</u>, but something I might call <u>caveat</u> <u>auditore</u> - let the auditor beware.

A second category of concern is the dominance of the regulatory environment. In the 1970s the eruption of congressional and regulatory oversight of the accounting profession produced much change - some of it valuable, much of it silly. We are approaching another period of additions to regulatory oversight, for a combination of political and social reasons. We are on the threshold of a second review of how the profession is governing itself and whether or not it needs more external governance. You have not yet even reached the first phase of concern, but I see some things in the British press that suggest to me that the Department of Trade and Industry is beginning to read about the Securities and Exchange Commission's activities and conclude that it has some of the same professional oversight responsibilities.

A third category of burdens upon our professional lives might be called 'the scope of duty'. Dean Prosser has given an explanation of the developing law of privity (or to whom the duty runs) in your environment. Clearly, the trend in Europe, the UK and elsewhere, is in the direction of the breaking down of the privity rule, the exposing of the accounting profession to wider and wider risk of claims. But even beyond the existing rule there are cases in the UK, Canada, Australia, and New Zealand, that are suggesting the question whether the exposure of the accounting profession merely to those whose reliance is foreseeable is wide enough? What is the position of an open market purchaser of a security? Is he really foreseeable as a potential user of financial statements? Do we have a whole new classification of risk that is being brought down on the head of the profession? In the USA, I fear that this is really a lost cause as far as the profession is concerned.

Let me describe a relatively recent decision of one of our major courts in the US involving something called the Panzirer case.[1] Mrs Zelda Panzirer was driving on a vacation through New England with her husband; she happened to be reading the Wall Street Journal and saw an article which touted the prospects for United Artists stock. She stopped the car at a public phone, called her broker and bought some United Artists stock. She had never seen the financial statements, much less the audit report; and neither had her broker. The Court of Appeals upheld her right to sue the auditor on the grounds of the efficient market hypothesis, the assumption that the auditor makes a contribution to the quality of information that makes its way into the public domain and consequently the price reflects the underlying financial statements and the work of the auditor. The allegations here were that United Artists should have had a 'going concern' qualification in the report issued prior to that Panzirer event, whereupon the stock would not have been touted in the Wall Street Journal and Mrs Panzirer would not have purchased, _ergo_ she would not have lost, _ergo_ she can sue the auditor. This is representative of what is becoming mainstream thinking based upon this efficient market hypothesis. So our scope of duty is becoming virtually limitless, it appears to extend to anyone who can allege a loss that bears the slightest kind of consequential relationship to something we touched in a professional capacity.

A fourth area that affects our degree of risk and is beyond our control is the state of the stock market: the volatility of our market as a whole and the volatility of given industries. It is almost unbelievable what has happened in the last 8 years to the auto industry, for example; it is very hard to try to predict how your audit report will be seen 2 or 3 years later. We are experiencing an explosion of tender offers and take-overs, each of which produces burdens and risks for the profession. There is no higher risk audit anywhere in the world than the purchase audit, or the pre-take-over audit. The technology of litigation is so well developed in the US that a standard check list of an astute acquiring company contains the question whether or not an asset acquired in the transaction might be a cause of action against the former company's auditor.

We are burdened by the volume and size of the bankruptcy problems of our economy, and we are worried by a steady level of fraud, either fraud by senior management on the public at large, or more recently a series of frauds committed by divisional management on the corporation, having as its objective the satisfying of sales and profitability goals, the enlargement of bonuses and the like. That has become a particularly difficult problem because it tends to happen below the materiality thresholds of audit examinations of consolidated statements.

Another category of event or development in the US that puts pressure on our profession is the emerging need for predictive skills in the conduct of an audit. I suggest that the traditional view of an historically-based audit examination and report is no longer representative of the North American scene. Although we have not legislated a change, the needs of the market place and the important facts about the financial statements are shifting. We have to deal with the consequence of increasingly long-term massive contracts. We have to try to focus on what will be the future pension burden of our clients, particularly the unfunded portions of it. We have to evaluate the adequacy of hedging in increasingly sophisticated investment programmes; Drysdale Securities and Marsh McClelland did not do that very well, and the audit profession is subject to the question: 'where were the auditors when those haemorrhages occurred to the client?'.

As a profession, we need to focus sharply on the short-term viability of companies. Penn Square, United American Bank, Johns Manville, Baldwin United and, most recently, the Chartered Companies are all major cases that represent bankruptcy liquidation or other winding up processes. All of them occurred within a matter of months, sometimes within weeks, of the issue of clean audit opinions. In our environment with 'going concern' qualification requirements, that ought not to be possible. It surely cannot be true that the auditing profession has failed that regularly to do something that it has the capacity to do if it exercises its judgement well. What we have to recognise is that in some areas (long-term contracts, pension benefits, hedged investments, viability examinations and sovereign debt) the actions that may arise from our audit reports have very little to do with historical data, but almost everything to do with prospective circumstances, many of them beyond our control and for which we have almost no tools and skills. We do not train in prospective judgements, we have not developed standards and skills to go along with it, and we are finding the world shifting faster than the technology needed to put us in a better position.

Another category of problem are the punitive statutes referred to by Peter Christie. Let me highlight this by talking about the Racketeering Influenced and Corrupt Organizations Act (RICO).[2] This is a federal law that is a classic American piece of logic that you will probably not have to encounter here. In the mid-1970s Congress decided that we needed additional civil and criminal penalties against the movement of organised crime into otherwise legitimate businesses. Congress put the price tag up for those caught, by arranging for criminal responsibility and treble the damages and costs of litigation for cases

where organised crime has caused commercial loss
to someone it has done business with. The
objective was reasonable, but there was a drafting
problem: how do you describe organised crime, what
is the universe you are trying to legislate
against? Congress found a solution that I think
would be beneath your standards of legislation;
they declared that organised crime is committed by
anybody who is convicted of two violations of
federal law within ten years. It took a while
for the plaintiffs' bar to catch on, but they have
now recognised that any violation of the
Securities Acts, of the mail fraud statutes, any
ordinary negligent abuse of state or federal law
(particularly in the commercial and accounting
categories) can count towards the qualifying two
violations. The result has been, within the last
three years, an abundance of claims against
accountants, brokerage firms and others.

One leading case involved a failed insurance
company in the mid-West that had been audited in
its last four years by three different
international accounting firms. The court-
appointed liquidator for that company, for which
organised crime had never been an issue, used a
RICO count to allege that those three audit firms
had caused $100 million in compensatory damages or
losses to the shareholders and policy holders of
the company; he added a gratuitous request for
standard punitive damages of $100 million, and a
RICO-based trebling penalty of an additional $300
million. That case has been in the courts for
almost three years, not even the Supreme Court has
seen fit to dismiss it as an inappropriate
application of RICO. We all have a large
portfolio of RICO cases; every one of ours is
brought by a bank, and none of them has anything
to do with organised crime. Most curiously, to
the best of my knowledge, there has never been a
RICO claim filed against someone who might really
have been involved in organised crime. Perhaps
that is a testament to the wisdom of the American
bar.

Another category of difficulty is the issue
that was discussed earlier: the professional

standards problem. There is one trend of issues
that suggests that it is not good enough to be
able to prove that you complied with GAAS and GAAP
if you should have known that something was not
being fairly communicated to the public. The
Continental Vending case[3] has been mentioned. In
that case, three partners of a Big Eight firm were
convicted of criminal charges. Experts from
six other Big Eight firms, including Robert
Trueblood, a senior member of the US profession,
testified for those partners and their actions,
but the jury still convicted them. The three
quickly received a Presidential pardon, and one
then became chief financial officer of a publicly
held company that my firm audited. The company
was sold a couple of years ago, and we are now the
defendant in a $30 million suit for having relied
upon that gentleman's representations concerning
the financial statements. I think we can prove
that he was as honourable in this latter episode
as he was when he was auditing Continental
Vending, but it will cost us something to do so.
    This leads to the difficult professional
issue: how can we, when we are already facing
this stressful professional environment, expect to
keep raising our own standards internal to the
firm if every time we amend our manuals, publish a
technical bulletin, address a difficult issue in
writing, when all of that is discoverable by a
potential opponent and usable against us? Yet
the profession cannot, and must not, stop raising
its sights and its standards. We must not be
defeated by these burdens to the point of not
developing responsibly, and we cannot communicate
in our size of operation without putting things in
writing. It is helpful, as Dean Prosser has
pointed out, to try to draft standards carefully
but this will not avoid all problems.
    The consequence of these events in the US is
significant; our insurance premiums have risen
greatly over a 10 or 12 year period, and we have
substantially higher "excesses". Our insurance
programmes have become more like catastrophe
protection than ordinary protection and that is
one of the market conditions that is potentially

repeatable here.   On top of these economic
consequences, there are the human and the
professional problems that it brings.   The human
trauma associated with being sued, particularly
when the business environment that you are living
in does not recognise suits as an ordinary part of
life, is enormous.   In the 1970s our firm alone
had three partners die of heart attacks within a
matter of three to four weeks after they or the
firm were sued in connection with one of their
principal accounts.   This has not happened again
for a number of years; it may just be a
coincidence, but I believe that the stress level
is highest when the phenomenon is newest.   If
there is anything that we can do to reach across
borders to help each other it is to suggest that
you establish a readiness to deal with the trauma
so that the pain level is not so high as it was
when we walked into it, innocent and abysmally
naive.

     In addition to the above problems there is
the professional disruption.   Consider the burden
of trying to manage a practice while significant
parts of your staff are absorbed in the
emotionally traumatic process of defending their
work, to say nothing of what can be done to an
office environment when a team of lawyers start
examining your working papers and expecting to be
accommodated at their schedule and not yours.
However, the biggest problem is to retain a sense
of proportion, the unanimity of effort that is
needed to manage a professional practice.   How
would you maintain that environment, for example,
in the Saxon case that I mentioned earlier, when
the partners had to go home and tell their
families that all their personal possessions
were, in effect, to be deposited in the court
house in New York to await the outcome of the
case?   That is a more dramatic example than
usual, but you cannot afford to buy enough
insurance such that every time you are sued you
can tell your partners that you have coverage to
protect them in the event of total loss.
Managing the risk component is difficult in that
environment; managing the practice so that it

remains productive and growth-oriented is even more difficult.

What can be done about these problems? First, we must deal with the "expectation gap". There are expectations of the profession that the world will make; we are expected to be more and more effective in detecting problems in financial statements. The Alberta Securities Commission in Canada recently held that an auditor should know that his work will be relied upon by a prospective investor, that reliance on the accuracy and veracity of a prospectus is fundamental to a healthy investing industry, and that the public perceives that an auditor will perform to a standard of professionalism, is independent of the issuer and will maintain and demonstrate objectivity of presentation. Thus, the auditor carries a grave responsibility in the nature of a 'public trust'. Those last two words are awesome because they imply a fiduciary responsibility. This goes beyond professional negligence responsibility, it shifts the burden of proof to show that you met your public trust, which is hard when things have gone awry. In commenting on that decision, a prominent barrister in Canada concluded that the courts would not take the same approach as the Commission.

That is fine enough for Canada, but the US Supreme Court earlier this month, in a case[4] involving Arthur Young on vastly different issues, threw in some gratuitous descriptions of the legal and accounting professions: the legal profession is there to advocate a client's cause; the accounting profession is there (in the unanimous verdict of our Supreme Court) as a public watchdog with a public trust, and the client relationship is _irrelevant_ to the responsibilities of the auditor. The consequences of that are frightening if that is indeed what our Supreme Court means. I hope that you can educate the members of your business and professional environments to the extent that you do not have to face those awesome implications.

The other side of the expectation gap is seen within the profession itself. We have some traditional attitudes and assumptions governing our work in much of the world. We rely upon our own sense of professional judgement and integrity, and we will normally close an audit with a self-satisfaction test. Unfortunately, we cannot always be right, especially in a volatile and complex financial community. Self-satisfaction will not be a defence, however genuinely held. Competence and integrity will not be enough, you will have to _demonstrate_ that you did all that you could, and that means that we must abandon several assumptions :

- We cannot afford to assume that we will not be sued. We must, as far as possible, conduct audit operations as if we had been sued once before. I have lived through the difference between a good auditor before and a good auditor afterwards, and if you can begin to perceive it in advance it will be easier for you.

- We have to abandon the assumption that no-one will ever read our working papers. Some of them _will_ be read. They will be read with a view to what they do not contain (do working papers show that you understood all of the issues involved and that you developed a logic trail to the conclusion that you reached) and, sometimes, they will be read more viciously for what they _do_ contain. Many people paid out much money in settling the Equity Funding litigation in the US. One of them was a Big Eight accounting firm that had never come near auditing Equity Funding or any of its related entities. However, it had done a consulting examination for a wholly separate client that at one time had considered and rejected an investment in Equity Funding. In the course of that consulting engagement an astute young man who was well down the line of responsibility wrote a note that said: "this sure looks like fraud to me". It cost a great deal for that firm, which had come no closer to Equity Funding than this, to deal with that undisciplined, uncorrected, albeit accurate, note on its working papers. The risk is of course that when your staff do make notes like that, they may just be right; and we will be expected to take action to protect the public, regardless of the context in which we develop such suspicions.

- We also have to abandon the assumption that good faith acceptance of a client's representations will never be challenged, particularly where we ask a question because something seems curious. If you stop with the client's acceptance and do not find additional support to make your conclusions logical, you are exposed thereafter.

- Further we have to abandon the assumption that our audit staff, particularly at the lower levels, are able to tell us at the partner level all that we need to know about the entity we are reviewing. A very wise colleague pointed out to me many years ago that the profession might not have got into so much trouble in the USA if it had not been for McKesson and Robbins in 1940.[5] A problem in McKesson and Robbins was the failure of a low level staff member of the audit firm to recognise that you could not move goods from Australia to San Francisco by lorry.

- Ultimately, we must abandon the assumption that third party confirmations supporting a client's figures dispel whatever suspicions of fraud we might otherwise have. In our environment the instances of multiple party fraudulent transactions are frequent and recurring. They recur where you least expect them; sometimes supplier confirmations and even bank confirmations turn out to be unreliable.

If there is any advice to be given it is that failure to appreciate the potential for risk and the ways of minimising that risk in your own conduct of practice, or failure to be disciplined by the need for defensive measures as you go about your work, are much more likely to cause you injury than are assaults by a client or by any third party.

A View from the USA

Notes

(1) <u>Zelda Panzirer v Emanuel L Wolf et al</u>, 663 F
     2d 365.
(2) Corrupt Organizations Act, 18 USC ss 1961-
     1968 (1982).
(3) <u>United States v Simon</u>, (1969) 425 F 2d 796.
(4) <u>United States v Arthur Young and Co et al</u>,
     104 S Ct 1495.
(5) SEC, ASR No 19, 1940.

Chapter Seven

THE UK POSITION NOW AND IN THE FUTURE : INTERNATIONAL INFLUENCES

Paul J Rutteman, CBE[*]

It was some 13 years ago that I became involved with this subject, when I was working with Carl Liggio on a problem concerning the Bahamas. He subsequently became our US firm's counsel, and I remember Carl suggesting that the US experience would be repeated in the UK. I responded that the UK is very different. At that time most of the US actions were class actions taken on a contingent fee basis. The laws of maintenance and champerty prevented that in the UK. It also seemed to me that the US accounting firms were a 'soft touch', because anyone could bring an action against a firm of accountants. They would then be involved in a tremendous amount of work, expense and legal fees, and not get a cent back, even if there was a successful defence. There was, thus, a temptation to settle early. Furthermore, the SEC was already attacking accountants to try to get consent decrees in order to improve the standards of the profession. Accounting firms were happy to agree not to do any wrong, without admitting that they had done any wrong in the first place. Carl Liggio was very much against that and, when the SEC took action against our firm in the Geotek case,[1] we

---

[*] This chapter is based on a transcript of a talk by Paul Rutteman, initially edited by Professor Nobes, and revised by Mr Rutteman.

defended it successfully - but how much cheaper to enter a consent decree!

That was a very different scene from the UK. I think there are still some significant differences. Rick Murray has told us that the US pattern has changed very much, to one where banks, liquidators, receivers and trustees are bringing the actions. I feel that UK banks are not likely to go to the same lengths, nor all liquidators. Banks are less keen to provide indemnities to receivers in the UK, and liquidators and receivers are careful about bringing actions if they are not sure of getting their money back. Nevertheless, as Peter Christie has shown, the UK situation has been deteriorating. You have only to look at the headlines on actions and settlements to realise that. It is true too that most settlements have been out of court. Some have come perilously close to court and it is interesting to observe the pressures in the City in such cases. One settlement was made, after pressure, a week before it was due to appear in court. The claim was some £5 million and the settlement was reported at £0.5 million. That was then the record. It is believed that the auditors of London and Counties Securities Ltd settled, without admitting fault, for £0.9 million. In the Isle of Man, there was recently a reported settlement approaching £10 million.[2]

As far as Continental Europe is concerned, they are saying what we were saying some 13 years ago. They perceive professional negligence claims as endemic to the English-speaking world. That has changed slightly; for example, in the Bieberhaus case[3] in Germany there was quite a large settlement, as I will mention later. So, it is interesting to see that Carl Liggio may have been right; such problems do move across borders. Indeed, in some cases a company in one country has brought an action across to another. The German example involved a UK purchaser in the first place, and there are American links to some major UK actions. So the position is bad, even if it is not quite as bad as on the other side of the

Atlantic.

I think, also, that our law is more protective. It is true that we have moved on from the <u>Candler v Crane Christmas</u> case[4] which said that only someone in a contractual fiduciary relationship could sue. We had Hedley Byrne,[5] but legal guidance (and the then current English Institute manual) suggested that Hedley Byrne was not as bad as it seemed at the time, and that we still had a similar position to the American one as set out in the Ultramares case,[6] when Judge Cardozo held that it would be wrong to expose auditors to potential liability 'in an indeterminable amount, for an indefinite time, to an indeterminate class'. I am sorry that those wise words are now history and that some of the advice that was in the Institute manual is now out of date and has been removed. The Hedley Byrne section of the manual formerly said that counsel's opinion was that a claim by an individual shareholder would not succeed in respect of loss suffered through his own investment decisions, made on the strength of misleading company accounts supported by an auditor's report containing negligent misrepresentation, since the purpose for which annual accounts are normally prepared is not to enable the individual shareholders to take investment decisions. Further, it was suggested that, even if practising accountants knew that the accounts would also form the basis of the client's assessments to tax, there would be no grounds for action by the Revenue. I suspect that we will not be relying on that any longer.

We have moved on; the Jeb Fasteners case[7] and the Twomax case,[8] which is going to appeal very shortly, must now be the basis of guidance. I think that accountants are now working on the assumption that the accounts on which they report will be used for whatever purpose a reader chooses. A few years ago we were debating the format of the audit report and to whom it should be addressed. Was it still right to address it to the members of the company? In the Netherlands the heading had been removed, and the Dutch profession holds that the accounts are for use by the world at large. Our conclusion was that we might retain a little protection by addressing the report to the members. I suspect that is too optimistic.

So, how can we protect ourselves legally? Can we obtain an indemnity from the client? In some countries which still use old UK company law this might be successful, but not now in the UK. Then, there is the question whether one can restrict the use of reports other than audit reports. You may try, but those reports can easily fall into other people's hands, and protection cannot be guaranteed. Furthermore, because of the Unfair Contract Terms Act, one cannot contract out of responsibility for negligence. So, disclaimers of an 'E and OE' nature may not give much protection.

My Institute's advice goes on to suggest that one should ensure that the terms of an engagement are absolutely clear. However, there remains the risk that litigants may not have seen the engagement letter because they relied on the report in a totally different context. There is also excellent guidance on avoiding giving snap advice or instant answers to questions, and on avoiding going beyond your expertise. Perhaps the most obvious guidance is to make sure that you secure your own quality control. If there has been a by-product of the legal problems over the last decade, it is an improvement of quality control within firms. However, competition is driving fees down fast; and at the same time our costs are rising substantially as a result of the quality control improvements. Quality control has to be applied right at the beginning. The best way to secure quality is to get the best people. Recruitment is very competitive; the 'milk round' at the universities is certainly producing the best candidates for the profession that we have ever seen. They are trained at enormous expense and supervised very carefully; they are getting considerable technical guidance and are taught to document everything carefully. Audit trails are now very clear and there are quality control reviews afterwards. That all costs a phenomenal amount of money.

The other aspect of quality control, which affects the clients in the weakest financial position, is that we have learned to watch for risky clients. These come in many forms. Clients who start off as low-risk clients can, in a period of recession, rapidly become high-risk clients. At that stage we tend to assess carefully just what the risks are and how to monitor them. The effect is that, as companies get into financial difficulties, their audit costs increase substantially. We put additional partners on to the job; staff are carefully selected for maximum experience at all levels; there is much double-checking and technical advice at all stages; and towards the end you will obviously try to predict the next 12 months, because we fear the unfortunate public perception that a clean audit report means that the company is safe for another 12 months. However, if you qualify your report when the company might have survived the next 12 months, you can be certain that it will not survive. That is disastrous. For these risky clients, we check cash flow projection, we look for sufficient working capital. These are areas where the more work you do, the more you can be challenged in the future for having got your assessment wrong.

Thus, litigation and quality control has to some extent led to defensive auditing. The higher costs hit hardest those in the greatest trouble. It has also led to protective language; quite often the auditor is trying to warn but is not able to do so succinctly for fear that it would further jeopardise the company. For he might well be sued for being too clear when the company might not have collapsed.

Let me now turn to the question of accounting standards. I note Dean Prosser's advice that we should not have accounting 'standards' but statements of guidance or normal practice. However, the result of this can be woolly accounting standards, and that helps no-one. I would like to see standards that are clear and that give some measure of protection, because if standards can be interpreted in different ways this also leads to great difficulty. These problems can also result in a cut back in accounting development. I will make a comparison with the States where, perhaps as a result of problems in the late 1920s and early 1930s, there is a tendency to treat historical costs as sacrosanct even though they may be meaningless. The reason may be a fear of revaluations. Rick Murray said that in the USA certain people are careful to do a purchase audit and to examine all the assets at the time of acquisition. This is happening in Europe too, and it is the revalued assets which are the first basis for a challenge. It would be a pity if we moved back to saying that historical costs at least have the virtue of certainty even if they may be meaningless. I hope we can go forward and try to make the accounts more useful to the user even if they are less certain and more vulnerable to attack.

Profit forecasts and cash flow projections are high risk areas. One thing is certain - profit forecasts will not be exact. Thus, the auditor is in the firing line. This is similar to the perception that an audit report guarantees the next 12 months, and some programme for educating the public is needed. We may also soon have problems on CCA. The profession is looking to include in the scope of the audit opinion the CCA information expected from large companies. Auditors would have to give opinion on rather more than they have in the past. The old attachment "prepared in accordance with SSAP 16" did not mean very much but, when CCA information is covered by a "true and fair" opinion, the auditor may be very much more vulnerable.

There is a risk that we could stop or delay some useful developments for fear of litigation. It would be sad if we became as defensive as the US medical profession, where if you go to the doctor for an aspirin you cannot get past the receptionist without having a blood test because there might be some other ailment that the doctor might otherwise miss. By giving the blood test he hopes to protect himself from future negligence claims.

As has been suggested, one of the reasons why auditors have been sued so frequently is the "deep pocket" syndrome. I was glad to hear the suggestion that directors might be expected to have more compulsory insurance. This leads us to the question whether auditors should have compulsory insurance? I think that is not very far off. The Law Society have it, and we have schemes that are not yet compulsory. The Gower Report envisages forms of self-regulation as part of which it may become incumbent on the profession to secure a similar system to the Law Society's. If there is a compulsory system, what sort of minimum requirement should we have? I believe that the basic schemes offered by our various Institutes do not provide sufficient protection without additional layers of cover. There have been several claims against small firms in excess of £1 million, whereas a typical cover, under the Institute's scheme, for a smaller firm is about half that. The examples I gave earlier were all claims well in excess of £1 million. Problems concerning a couple of bank scandals have led to the Manx government introducing a compulsory minimum insurance level of £10 million for auditors of banks in the Isle of Man, and £5 million for insurance company auditors. And that was set at what was regarded as a low level so as not to discriminate in favour of the larger firms. So levels of insurance have been far too low.

We have concentrated here on civil liability, the making good of the damages suffered by a plaintiff. However, there is also a public expectation that concerns self-regulation in a different sense. There was a clamour for a joint disciplinary scheme which is now being shown to work quite well. It reflects some of the better parts of what the SEC has been trying to do in the USA, ensuring that there is investigation of bad auditing or bad accounting, as uncovered in many cases by the DTI.

May I comment on the statement attributed to Ian Hay Davison concerning the nature of the international firm? There have been a few problems of this kind, some concerning Bahamian banks. A firm may sometimes argue that it is not really an international firm, even though all of its publications are labelled 'So and So, International'. It is difficult to hold out at one moment that you are one firm world-wide, but when it comes to legal action to hold that you are actually a series of separate partnerships using the same name. I think that will not work for very long, and I think that litigants will choose where the action can best be taken.

That brings me back to the case that I first worked on with Carl Liggio - the Koch v Vosko action.[9] This concerned a Bahamian company that received an audit report locally, and subsequently was purchased by an American company. The action was taken in the USA against the US firm on the basis that the report looked like a US report, even though it was made in the Bahamas. Eventually we won that case, but there is a lesson in that: what appears safe in the UK can have international ramifications because of the international nature of the firm. There have been many cases which stretch across borders. In the Cayman Islands, for example, there was a Latin-American bank settlement reported at $10.7 million which went across borders in terms of where the insurance lay.[10]

There is also the question of subsidiary auditors. It was originally a US idea that where you have a group of companies with subsidiaries across the world, only one auditing firm (which usually means one of the Big Nine) should carry out the audit. That idea has now spread to the UK, and there is good reason for it. There have been many cases where problems have arisen due to subsidiary auditors operating to different standards, which nevertheless resulted in the parent company auditor being sued because it had the deepest pocket. I suspect, therefore, that we will see a trend towards group auditors in Europe as well. For example, German companies have tended not to have the same world-wide associations nor world-wide consolidations. So they were less interested in who audited the foreign subsidiaries. However, Germany and other EEC countries will soon require world-wide consolidations.

Let me move on to another international aspect. We are facing the possibility of new problems resulting from EEC harmonisation. We have seen some aspects of our law having to change as a result of the Fourth Directive. The law now lays down certain principles and rules, making it more difficult to apply judgement to the overriding "true and fair view". The Accounting Standards Committee has obtained counsel's opinion on the meaning of the "true and fair view", in the context of whether ASC could say that it is necessary to provide CCA information in order to show a "true and fair view". ASC's legal advisors initially suggested that since the "true and fair view" was already included in the 1948 Act before CCA existed, a "true and fair view" could presumably exist without CCA information. However, counsel advised that the term can change its legal meaning over the course of time, in the same way that 'cruel' or 'poor' could. Thus, ASC could say that CCA was necessary and, if this view is generally accepted by professional accountants, the courts would agree. Furthermore, this recognised no contradiction in the situation that in Germany you are required to have a "true and fair view" and it cannot include CCA, whereas in the UK you would have to include CCA to show a "true and fair view". I wonder whether the European Court in Luxembourg would interpret the Directive in the same way.

The Second and Third Directives both require the auditors to report on valuations – the Second Directive, when consideration other than cash is given for the capital of a public company; the Third Directive, where there is a merger between two companies of a special kind found in continental Europe (a _fusion_), where the assets and liabilities of the company being merged are transferred into the survivor company, while the merged company disappears. The share exchange ratio has to be the subject of the auditor's scrutiny. These are areas of judgement and valuation which I foresee will lead to many disputes. Further, the Fifth Directive may cause difficulties in future. It appears that auditors will be liable for any wrongdoings on the same basis as the directors, the difference of course being that auditors may have the deeper pocket. Also, the auditors will have to give a long-form report, including a mention of any danger to the continuing existence of the company. The report would be sent to the supervisory board or to the non-executive directors, and would be available to shareholders. Thus, there is scope for anyone to say that there had been insufficient warning of imminent collapse, if there was no warning of financial danger in the auditors' long-form report. All these points will increase the risk of litigation.

Let me turn to what is happening in some other EEC countries. The problems we have discussed will eventually reach those countries also. In the meantime, German auditors are in a splendid position. They have a limitation of liability in respect of any statutory audit work to a maximum of DM 0.5 million. We have tried unsuccessfully to persuade the Commission to draft a harmonising Directive. On this basis, in Germany there is further apparent protection in that most audits are carried out by limited companies. However, I do not think that helps much because the partners' personal assets may well be protected from a claim which exhausts the assets of the company but it sinks the company, and I cannot see any major firm being able to continue in business after this. Insurance in Germany is arranged through the Institut's scheme. The minimum cover required is DM 0.5 million per case or DM 2.5 million per annum. (That seems to be based on up to 5 cases a year!)

This should all be seen in the context of a country which has had a low claims experience, until cases like the Bieberhaus affair emerged, which I mentioned earlier. This was a case where a UK store group purchased a German store group and engaged a firm of accountants to look at the accounts. It subsequently transpired that the accounts were not right. The court held that this was not an audit but an acquisition report and that there was therefore no statutory protection for the auditors. The result was an initial award of damages of DM 5 million and further claims to the order of DM 35 million. That was the first German case of that order of magnitude.

In France there have also been changes that could lead to more actions in the future. The COB (Commission des opèrations de Bourse) is now controlling listed companies quite well. It has the power to remove incompetent auditors after a suitable investigation. That it has done so suggests that there have been problems and that the former auditors may be liable for civil damages. So far, claims experience is not that high in France. However, the French are acutely aware of developments elsewhere and of the need to improve quality. They are now setting up a system of peer review which looks as if it may become compulsory. The idea has been imported from the USA where it was adopted by the profession as a defensive measure against the threat of imposed reviews. Originally, the European profession argued vigorously against the peer review system being extended to non-US offices of the major firms. We and the French were active in resisting it. I am still not convinced by the case for peer review, having looked at the costs, which are high and which can only be recovered through charging clients.

There are other aspects of regulation in France which are much more unattractive. The auditor has responsibilities additional to those he has in the UK, some of which it looked as if we might have to import via the Fifth Directive. In France the auditor has a quasi-judicial role. He has to denounce to the authorities any criminal acts or any breaches of law that he sees which are of a financial nature, presumably including breaches of exchange control regulations, for example. There have been problems in the past where an auditor has issued an opinion and then

97

tried to withdraw it after discovering it was wrong, but unfortunately not being able to get back all the copies. In cases like that the auditor has found himself before the criminal court for issuing a false opinion. He has little defence because the old and new opinions are extant, and the first was obviously wrong. This has resulted in at least one senior French accountant being given a suspended sentence. These are the sorts of difficulties which I hope are not imported into the UK through EEC law. As you may imagine we are doing our best to make sure that does not happen. The other development in France is compulsory insurance; and in this it appears that we may have to follow the French.

In the Netherlands, the recession has left a number of companies in difficulties; a large mortgage bank recently collapsed. There is an organisation there called SOBI which is a pressure group, claiming to protect the public, that looks at such companies' accounts. Its leader, Peter Lakeman, has brought actions before the Enterprise Court on a number of occasions, and he claims a certain amount of success. He has tried, for example, to get the Enterprise Court to take action against auditors where a receiver failed to.[11] The Enterprise Court has no power to award damages, but it can order accounts to be withdrawn and be drawn up afresh. In some cases, accounting principles have been at issue. To take one technical area, in one case SOBI said that there should be no deferred tax assets in the accounts (although under Dutch accounting principles there can be). The Court held that it does not make sense to have a deferred tax asset, so now there is some question as to the status of codified Dutch accounting principles.

The Fourth Directive has meant that a large number of companies must have a proper audit for the first time. This is particularly relevant for Belgium (and Germany). There has therefore been a re-organisation in the accounting profession, with government help because the profession in these countries is under government supervision. There has been an attempt in Belgium in the course of re-organisation to secure limited liability for the auditor. However, since at the same time the profession was arguing that it was a 'liberal' profession, the government responded that a liberal profession must suffer unlimited liability. There is also a very low fee structure. This arises because in Belgium only listed companies had to have a real audit; other companies had audits but they could be carried out by unqualified individuals or by non-independent auditors - even by the financial controller of the company. How do you move from one sort of compulsory audit to another sort of compulsory audit, and raise the fees to an appropriate level for a real audit? This will lead to tremendous pressure, and auditors will find it difficult to resist short cuts. So Belgium may move from a low-risk to a high-risk country.

To conclude, my suspicion is that the law in this country is not going to help us. I agree that the duty of care in future is likely to be interpreted as in the Jeb Fasteners case,[12] which means that we will owe a duty of care to anyone who could reasonably be foreseen to be a user of the accounts, and we thus have to accept that anyone may rely on audited accounts. I fear that limited liability status for auditors is a forlorn hope, and might not help anyway. I am concerned about the 'deep pocket', and I think this will lead to more actions against UK auditors. All of this is bad news.

I believe that the level of cover is too low at the moment for many of the smaller firms, and that there may be a fee increase across the board. Anyone who plans to do without cover because it is too expensive will find it much more expensive not to have any. However, it must become clear that people other than auditors are most usually responsible for problems, perhaps the directors. That is not yet happening in the courts, but they may be becoming more skilled at distinguishing fault.

I am deeply concerned by the trend in acquisitions where high prices are paid but things do not work out, followed by litigious shots at a number of different targets. I have a case in mind where a UK company paid £7 million for a company.[13] The company's profits were expected to be £1.4 million but turned out to be £1 million, and the assets were found to be overstated. The effect of that was to try to recover most of the £7 million in different ways : action against a merchant bank with respect to the profit forecast; and against the auditors of the acquired company; there was an ex gratia payment of £400,000 from the reviewing auditors (the other claims being in the order of £3.5 million and £3 million). It is interesting how close the numbers were to the price that was paid in the first place. I fear that we will see more of this. I hope that the courts may in future decide that the acquisitions might have been made anyway. I fear that this problem will spread to Europe.

I would like to see compulsory cover introduced throughout the profession, and I think it will happen. Finally I do not think it is all bad news; the quality of the profession has risen rapidly over the last few years. I think we are recruiting the best people, and there is no better protection than quality people.

Notes

SEC v Geotek Resources Fund (1975), 518 F 2d 1198.

Creditors of the Isle of Man Bank International Finance and Trust Corp v Midgely Snelling, in Accountancy Age, 27.10.83 and 10.5.84.

Mobel Hubner v Peat Marwick Mitchell, W German Appeal Court, 1978.

Candler v Crane Christmas and Co (1951), 2KB 164.

Hedley Byrne and Co Ltd v Heller and Partners (1964), AC 465.

Ultramares Corporation v Touche et al (1931), 174 NE 441.

Jeb Fasteners Ltd v Marks Bloom and Co (1981), 3 All ER 289.

Twomax Ltd v Dickson, McFarlane and Robinson (1983), SLT 98.

Koch Industries Inc v Irwin Lyon Vosko and Arthur Young and Co (1974), 494 F 2d 713.

0   Pannell Fitzpatrick sued. Financial Times, 24.2.81.

1   SOBI v Tilburgsche Hypotheek Bank, in Financieel Dagblad 14.9.83 and Volkskrant 14.9.83.

2   As note 7.

3   Pentos v Singer Friedlander.

PART III

Chapter Eight

QUESTIONS AND ANSWERS[*]

TOPIC A.   TO WHOM DUTY IS OWED/SCOPE OF DUTY

1. Question to Prosser :

One of the problems that accountants face
is that they cannot always foresee who will
ultimately take possession of reports that
were given in a certain set of circumstances.
They may find their way into the hands of
others to be used for another purpose.   For
example, an advisory report may be done for a
company which is taken over within a matter of
months.   Yet, if one hedged one's work around
with disclaimers, it would become anodyne and
sterile.   To what extent would the courts
recognise the circumstances of the particular
report?

Reply :

I am pessimistic about that.   I think
that the courts would not be much impressed,
for example, if an accountant said that he did
not foresee that a particular person would put
in a takeover bid and was going to use the

---

* The transcript of these questions and answers
from the conference has been prepared by C W
Nobes.

accounts.   They would say that if you know
that there is a takeover coming, you will owe
some duty to those interested in that way;
and, since one knows that bids of that kind
are part of the commercial world, that is a
broad category of person who will be
interested.   They are not going to look
merely to the particular people, they are
going to look at categories of people and,
therefore, it will not be just the existing
lender or the intending lender, it will be any
possible lender;   it will not be the existing
investor or the intending investor, it will be
any possible investor.   However, of course,
there would be a limit somewhere;   if it was
put to some really specific use, perhaps in
relation to some particular contract, then one
could say that that is getting beyond what one
could have had in mind.   But I think it is
very wide.

2.   Question to Murray :

In the Panzirer case, were actions taken
against any other person than the auditor?

Reply :

The case was brought, I believe,
exclusively against the auditor;   it was
brought by one of the highly developed
specialists of the plaintiffs' bar who could
readily perceive that United Artists itself
was having financial difficulties   and that
the return on investment of the plaintiff's
time in suing them might be low.   It was a
manifestation of the 'deep pocket' phenomenon.
The testimony of the plaintiff was that the
only thing she had ever heard about United
Artists was that article, which would not have
existed if a going concern qualification had
been rendered.   The fact that there was an
intermediary, the reporter, did not enter into

the case.

3. Question to Murray :

My question concerns accountants'
liability as opposed to auditors' liability.
It is very common for auditors to give
additional advisory services to their audit
clients.   Therein lies a growing danger
because the auditor, in his concern to give
good service to his client, is sometimes
induced to add credence to representations his
client is seeking to make.   This particularly
happens where finance is sought.

Imagine an audit client with bookkeeping
problems who also has a cash flow problem.
He asks the audit firm to get his records
straight, and the auditors work day and night
to do so and produce some interim accounts for
internal use.   They are very cannie auditors,
so the interim statements do not have the
audit firm's name on them.   Also they do not
write an audit report, but they do write a
disclaimer that points out that certain of the
assets have not been verified.   Suppose that
the client   puts the document in front of
another company which he knows has funds to
make available.   He states that it was drawn
up by his auditors, well-known to the company
he is approaching.   There is nothing to say
the auditor prepared those statements except
the word of the client, so the financier
telephones the auditor.   Unless the auditor
is very careful at this point, anything he
says that implies confirmation may render him
liable to the third party making the enquiry.
In these cases the problem lies not in written
material but in some alleged oral
representation.   How can auditors safeguard
themselves in these circumstances?

Reply :

I would have a fairly pessimistic view of this in America. We cannot prevent that kind of event because we cannot train our staff to have a mouthful of disclaimers every time they speak; and if we did successfully train them we would not have a practice left to worry about.

We have an even more advanced problem in the US, concerning non-audit services including unaudited financial statements, limited reviews, or something not involving audit expertise, such as consulting or tax. Whatever the product, if we are accused of not having done as well as we could, it does not solve the problem to claim that it was not what we were engaged to do. The case will be tried on the theory that the firm holds itself out as having a broad range of skills, including audit skills and procedures and a whole range of other skills. If we had expertise in our house that would have been able to help correct whatever the abuse was that we are being sued for, we would find it difficult to explain why we did not apply it successfully, even though that expertise goes beyond the nature of the service or the engagement contract.

Reply by Rutteman :

It is true that accountants very frequently assist clients to seek finance and it is normal practice to prepare cash flow forecasts or even a presentation package for the bank. Now, what can you do and what is actually done? I think the first case is to make sure that everything is in writing. It must be made clear just what the purpose is and what the limitations are, what you have done and what you have not done. One must make clear to the bank how far the figures are based on soft information which has not been verified or is not capable of verification. Further, make sure that you do not give snap advice and that you put things in writing afterwards.

Reply by Morrison :

In the hypothetical case discussed, perhaps the auditor made a mistake in not asking his client whether he could discuss the unaudited accounts with him before he discussed them direct on the telephone with the financier. If he buys that bit of time and knows what to do, he may be in a better position.

Reply by Prosser :

It is unreal to suggest that people will not go beyond the terms of their engagement or the terms of their audit function. Equally, it is unreal to suggest that people will not give verbal advice. However, it is much better to have the engagement in tight terms so that you can at least start by claiming that you said nothing on that topic, supported by your terms of engagement. Equally, try to advise in writing and try to confirm verbal advice afterwards.

Reply by Murray :

I would encourage the use of written disciplines for communications wherever you can. However, a few months ago we gave a draft opinion on tax forecasts for a shelter promotion, indicating in our report that it was draft. It was unsigned; it was subject to the receipt of additional information; and it was specifically declared to be usable only by the promoter for his own advisory purposes and not to be reproduced or shared with anyone else or relied upon for any purpose. Whereupon the caveat paragraph was removed and 40,000 copies distributed around the country. And the promoter sued us!

4. Question to Murray :

    Returning to the efficient market hypothesis, are you saying that the judiciary accept it?

    Reply :

    Yes, partly because it helps one to grapple with the myriad factors involved. It developed not out of the Panzirer case but from cases of the 1970s where class actions were being pursued by thousands of investors. This threatened the courts with endless hearings to determine whether each one of those thousands of people actually saw the financial statements or relied upon the audit report. The courts' reaction was that the number of cases was unthinkable, but that to throw all the cases out was also unthinkable; thus the efficient market hypothesis was very useful.

TOPIC B.   QUALITY OF CARE OWED

5. Question to Prosser :

    Could you expand on the point you made about the perceived ability of the client to whom you are giving advice? You gave the example of the specialist lawyer who, when advising a client who is totally a lay person, would have a wider responsibility. In the advisory field, the method of presentation and even the actual advice that you give cannot help but be conditioned by the people that you are advising; group A would be well competent to implement this particular scheme, whereas you feel that group B would not. The advice is written in particular circumstances at a particular time. It may be addressed to the directors Bloggs plc but it is, in fact, written with specific individuals in mind. A statutory audit opinion is couched in predetermined words but once one moves into advice, there is a lot of individuality.

Reply :

If the advice is given because you think the recipients are inadequate, and you would have given different advice if they were more competent, I agree that you probably cannot put in the report : "If you were a bit brighter we would tell you to do something else". I do not think you should really try. On the other hand, I think I would be cautious enought to make sure that there was something to that effect on my file, because I do not see how you can limit it otherwise. This ties in with what I was saying about evidence; that, without trying to plan litigation in everything one does, one does want to have good in-house records.

6. Question to Prosser :

What is the position where companies are to be wound up and at some date before that a firm of accountants has given a report which appears to suggest that all is well? It surprises me that more trouble does not come from this source for us as a profession. How do you see the liability of accountants when lenders and shareholders do not do things that they might have done had the accountants given warnings of events that, with hindsight, many of us could have seen by, for example, calculating a few ratios?

Reply :

I have said that I feel that the courts are likely to see a need for the accountant to give a positive warning; in other words, for the accountant not just to leave the interpretation of a report to its readers, but to comment. However, while I fear that the courts would do that, it seems to me to be wrong of them because the normal engagement would not be a forecasting function. Is the function of an audit report to be a commentary on the entire year or merely a statement at the final stage, and is it meant to be a commentary on the next year as well? In particular, you do get hints of the court's expecting it to have this kind of warning function, to be a forward looking document rather than just a narrative document. How one controls that I do not know; whether, for example, one can limit it in terms of the known forms of engagement.

7. Question to Prosser :

You mentioned the case of architects who had admitted that they had ignored or violated the rule because in their view the rule was wrong. Is it enough to argue that you personally think the rules wrong, or have you got to find others who will support you? In other words, does there have to be some indication that there is another accepted practice?

Reply :

You do not need to go as far as showing that there is another accepted practice, you do not need to generalise it as much as that. In the case that I mentioned earlier (<u>Kelly v Edinburgh Corporation</u>), one could claim that there was another accepted practice and a fairly universal one. It concerned the form of glass used in balconies on high rise flats, and the size that was acceptable and so on. In my view, you do not need to show that there is anyone else following your practice, but you would have to have the most marvellous reputation if you were really going to get away with saying : "I am out of step with the whole of the rest of the brigade but I'm right". However, the case is quite comforting for the professional who has the guts to say it, because it is accepted that rule-making is done by committees who are trying to find out what the best thinking is. Thus, if rules are always in a state of change, it follows logically that somebody must be ahead of his time rather than behind the times. However, it would be a hard task if you were really the only one who tried it. It has happened in medical cases where there has been a given way of operating which is universally accepted and yet a doctor tries an experimental technique. One could say that he is using his patient as a guinea pig, but that is how progress is made. Even if he could not point to many other people in the world who used that particular technique, he could get another doctor to say that it was reasonable.

8. Question to Prosser :

       What about the man who does what the rules require and yet is alleged to be culpable of negligence?

Reply :

       I do not think I know of such cases. In some medical cases, there are indications by the courts that even a generally accepted practice, which I think would include a stated practice, might be held negligent if the court reckoned the profession was letting their clients down. However, while that has been said in passing, I do not think I know of any case where compliance with the rule has still left you negligent.

Reply by Murray :

In the USA, compliance with recognised profession-wide standards is not a secure defence; it is certainly better than having no such defence but it is not the end of the enquiry process. And we are developing rapidly a judicial recognition where, particularly among the larger accounting firms, we have our own sets of standards and practices which are elevated above the profession-wide norm. This is how the profession-wide norm improves; so any difference between the profession's rules and the given firm's rules almost inevitably means that the latter is higher. However, there is a consistent trend of decisions that say that you can be held responsible for failing to meet your own internal requirements, even though those requirements are above the profession's and even though you can demonstrate that you satisfied the profession's. What would a British court do?

Reply by Prosser :

I cannot think of any example of this. In principle, you would be allowed to fall below your own normal high standards provided you still kept above the reasonably competent practitioner in the requisite field, and provided it is not a matter where you are holding yourself out as the specialist. I think that our courts would not impute liability on that. However, the other professions would be unlikely to have organised themselves to the extent of having formulated rules or to be on a big enough scale for it to happen. One could imagine architects having their own internal building standards which might be different within one firm. I think our courts would be reluctant to accept that the professional who sets himself an unusually high standard is liable, unless he has really written that high standard into his particular contract.

9. Question to Prosser :

Was it not in Continental Vending case that, despite many professionals saying that the auditors did indeed abide by generally accepted principles, the judge said that there are times when a professional might have to rise above that?

Reply :

Yes, that is a case where it was indicated that they would have to rise above the standard practice. I think the courts would do that. Whether they would hold you to a stated higher practice is another matter.

10. Question to Murray :

You mentioned that you will be held to a standard based on the ability to apply any in-house expertise to any issue. One of the current issues is the adequacy of reserves for insurance companies. Some major accounting firms have separate actuarial staff; how does this affect the case?

Reply :

This is not an abstract question. We have an actuary department. We have incorporated in our own manuals for auditing insurance companies the proposition that, given our in-house expertise, we may not naively rely upon an independent actuary's determination submitted by an insurance company client. First our own department

115

must advise the audit partner that all is appropriate. We have two actions pending in which there are allegations that we did not properly exercise our own independent skills to detect failings which turned out to be serious in actuarial determinations. I anticipate that the AICPA will move towards the conclusion that auditors have a responsibility here just as we do in the tax area, where we cannot rely upon an independent expert.

We would probably have had an easier time if we had not had in-house actuaries. However, that is not the same thing as saying we ought not to have an in-house actuarial capacity, because it ignores the cases where the use of that capacity has saved us from difficulties.

11. Question to Murray :

If in the USA you feel it necessary to mention in your audit manual that one cannot rely on outside actuaries, what does this imply about your UK firm's insurance company clients when you have a world-wide firm and world-wide manuals?

Reply :

I can only look to the wisdom of Mr Hay Davison, referred to earlier (ch 5).

12. Question to Prosser :

It was suggested that a court would hold that, if it was possible to carry out certain tests, you should have done so. However, reports usually have to be produced to a timetable, and it is not always possible to do

everything that you would like. To what
extent would the court recognise such time
pressures?

Reply :

I certainly think it would be relevant
that one was under time pressures, and I can
think of other contexts in which that has been
fully understood. In particular, for
example, in medical cases, a doctor acting
under time pressures cannot do all that he
would do at leisure and this is accepted as
one of the inputs into judging what he ought
to have done. However, if you had missed out
a standard procedure because of time, that is
dangerous. You are in a cleft stick : it
is dangerous to admit that you have not done
something you should have done and it is
dangerous not to admit it. However, in
medical cases, it is not only emergency action
that may be considered but every simple
pressure of work. The latter may not weigh
very heavily but it is seen as a relevant
consideration that a man in a hurry for
understandable reasons will do different
things from a man not in a hurry. However,
you would not get away with omitting anything
central.

Reply by Murray :

The question gives sharp focus to an
issue discussed this morning : do society and
the courts still accept a distinction between
error and negligence, or between an
expectation that is not fulfilled and
negligence? Most courts in the USA still
subscribe to that distinction. They do not
yet hold that any professional, particularly
not an accountant or auditor in the complexity
of our environment, is liable every time
things turn out badly. A typical case in US
litigation would involve the auditors being
able to demonstrate that the audit programme

was properly designed for the circumstances, met the professional requirements and was carried out in accordance with its intention to an appropriate degree. Thus the auditor would claim innocence. The plaintiff, knowing what went wrong, can show that if you had taken just one more step, not a thousand more steps to cover every possibility but just this one, all would have been well. Working backwards, there appears to be such a natural trail of logic leading to that one thing you did not do, that it is very tempting for a judge or a jury to conclude that either your programme or your execution was flawed. The conclusion is tantamount to a blurring of the distinction between error and fault, even though in theory nobody subscribes to that. Hindsight is at its most terrible when it comes to litigation of this nature. I hope that a judge would reject that but I am frightened that a jury might not.

In our $30 million loss, the jury was found to have been most influenced by a simple proposition (impressed upon them throughout the trial) that, if the auditors had made one ten cent phone call to a given individual and asked a question that seemed obvious with hindsight, he might have told you the truth (despite being a participant in the fraud) and that would have unravelled the whole scheme.

13. Question to Prosser. :

Normally it is held that trying to detect error and fraud is a spin-off of auditing. Are you suggesting that it should now be a major aim?

Reply :

I think you would be ill-advised to treat it as a main aim. Nevertheless, the courts have shifted towards saying that one must be suspicious, particularly of the possibility of mistake, and quick to identify hints of fraud. I doubt whether it is really right to act as if every set of accounts is liable to include fraudulent items, because that seems to depart from common sense.

TOPIC C. ACCOUNTING STANDARDS

14. Question to Prosser :

You seem to be saying that perhaps we are promulgating too many rules, regulations and standards. Does this mean a halt to standards because this may increase liability? However, some authorities are suggesting that auditing is no longer just an off-shoot of accounting but a profession on its own, and that the auditors must declare their standards and their postulates. Is there a middle path?

Reply :

I see it as inevitable and desirable that there should be widely stated standards covering great detail. So I am not saying "stop". However, I think it is a matter of draughtsmanship how one expresses them. I think in many of these matters they should be expressed as standards rather than rules; guidelines rather than requirements; statements of normal practice rather than, assertions of necessary practice. It is a matter of not overstating them; partly so that they can be more easily changed as well as departed from.

15. Question to Rutteman :

Is it possible that accounting standards may gain the force of law, as in Canada?

Reply :

I would like to see the Canadian system introduced over here but the chance of that happening is remote because Parliament is very reluctant to delegate legislation to outside bodies. There is only one exception to that so far, and it concerns the Stock Exchange. Recently, because of EEC Directives on the admission and listing particulars of securities, the Stock Exchange has now been given rule-making powers which Parliament might not otherwise have been willing to give. However, the Exchange is perhaps an institution rather than a profession.

TOPIC D. NUMBER OF CASES AND CASES FOUGHT

16. Question to Prosser :

Are you able to confirm the growth in the number of liability cases in your own work? When companies go into liquidation, will there be a crowd of vultures picking off the accountants?

Reply :

There is evidence to show that this is happening to some extent. The case law was very lean for a long time but more do seem to be pressing through to litigation. Some settle out of court. Scotland alone is too small to make any generalisation easy; I have had or been aware of several in the last couple of years. There is the Twomax case; there is one called Oliver v Douglas, part of

which has now settled out of court, concerned
with reliance on what one might have regarded
as fairly out of date material leading to a
supplier going on supplying.   I get the
impression that it probably is increasing, if
not yet flooding.

17. Question to Murray :

We get the impression that, in the 1960s
and 1970s,   the large US firms chose to
defend many cases irrespective of cost.   Do
you think that was the right decision and
will it continue in the 1980s?

Reply :

In the early 1970s we did not defend
every case.   There was a period when,
stimulated in part by underwriters, the
profession frequently settled out of court
because of the proposition that defending
costs more than settling.   We thereby built
up an expectation in the rather narrow
community of the bar that was specialising in
suing accountants.   The second phase was the
necessity to remove that expectation because
it puts the profession in great danger.   The
burden of resistance had to fall to the large
firms who were in a better position to take
the risks than a smaller firm would have been.
Thus a pattern of resistance developed.   It
certainly would not be fair to say that every
case is defended to the limit; there are cases
that ought to be settled and there arè
payments that ought to be made, and there are
some doubtful circumstances where prudence
suggests that when a favourable settlement
opportunity arises it should be taken.   But
the number of litigated cases has been on the
increase; there have been cases taken to
juries and, despite the uncertainties of that,
the larger firms in the US have done rather

well in defence.   More than half the cases
that   are   litigated   have   been   wholly
victorious.   And, although the activity level
is increasing and the courts are developing a
continuing set of new rules that do not make
it any easier, the technology of defence is
getting better too.   I certainly agree with
the proposition that we must continue to
manifest that kind of resistance.

As for hindsight, I would do the same
thing on 13 of our cases but differently on
one.   The one, which was the first that I
inherited in office, was something called US
Financial which we did take to trial.   The
client had not been particularly significant
as a client but when it became a law suit it
became very significant.   At one time we
faced roughly $400 million in pending claims
from banks and shareholders, which was
whittled down to one set of $30 million of
claims from banks.   We took the case to trial
because the other options were not attractive;
the case was tried for nine months before a
jury.   The plaintiff's first witness was our
audit partner, who spent seven solid weeks
testifying.   To his credit, though we lost
the entire $30 million, he remains a partner
with us.   No one would want to go through
that kind of torture.   The jury, after what
we thought was a reasonably successful trial,
took 20 minutes to conclude that we were in
the wrong and another eight days calculating
the damages.   I hope that we have become more
astute but we will never be able to eliminate
the potential for every large trial producing
that kind of result.

18. Question to Murray :

Is it possible that regulatory pressures
are lessening in the USA?

Reply :

Regulatory pressures were tending to diminish in the early years of the Reagan administration. Deregulation was affecting the securities field as well as others. However, several factors, including election pressure and the impact of some surprising major company failures for which scapegoats are necessary, have recently regenerated an environment where regulatory oversight hearings in Congress are likely and where there is pressure on the SEC to justify why it is not taking a harsher line with the accounting profession. Coupled with that is the continuing difficulty of the Financial Accounting Standards Board to give birth to other than mice for its mountainous efforts, and the accumulating feeling that the development of accounting principles through the FASB may not ultimately be satisfactory. Thus, 1984 and 1985 may be like 1977 and 1978.

FURTHER READING

1   Rupert M Jackson and John L Powell, Professional Negligence, Sweet and Maxwell, 1982.
2   Michael J Pratt, Auditing, Longman, 1983.
3   Jonathan R H H Pockson, Accountants' Professional Negligence - Developments in Legal Liability, Macmillan, 1982.
4   Lee, T A, Company Auditing : Concepts and Practices, Institute of Chartered Accountants of Scotland, 1972.
5   K M Stanton and A M Dugdale, "Recent Developments in Professional Negligence", 1 to 5, New Law Journal, December 1981 to April 1982.
6   Clifford Baxter, "New Professional Negligence Liability Judgement - An Auditor's Nightmare", Accountancy, August 1981.
7   Alan G Davison, "Auditors' Liability to Third Parties for Negligence", Accounting and Business Research, Autumn 1982.
8   T J Bailey, "Negligent Statements and the Reasonable Foresight Test", New Law Journal, July 15, 1982.
9   Allan Hutchinson and Derek Morgan, "Snail Tales - A Golden Trail", New Law Journal, May 27, 1982.
10 Sally P Gunz, "A Case of Negligence : A Professional Whodunit", CA Magazine, November 1983.
11 Institute of Chartered Accountants in England and Wales, Guidance for Members in Practice, November 1983.
12 Roy Chandler, "Auditors' Liability - Recent Developments", Accountant, January 12, 1984.
13 Henry R Jaenicke, The Effect of Litigation on Independent Auditors, Research Study No 1, Commission on Auditors' Responsibilities.

INDEX OF CASES

Index of Cases

Index of Cases